SURRENDERED & UNAFRAID

Fedd Books
P.O. Box 341973
Austin, TX 78734
www.thefeddagency.com

Published in association with The Fedd Agency, Inc., a literary agency.

Unless otherwise noted, all scripture quotations are taken from THE HOLY BIBLE, NEW INTERNATIONAL VERSION®, NIV® Copyright © 1973, 1978, 1984, 2011 by Biblica, Inc.® Used by permission. All rights reserved worldwide.

Scripture quotations marked NLT are taken from the Holy Bible, NEW LIVING TRANSLATION, copyright © 1996, 2004, 2015 by Tyndale House Foundation. Used by permission of Tyndale House Publishers, Inc., Carol Stream, Illinois 60188. All rights reserved.

Scripture quotations marked NASB are taken from the New American Standard Bible® (NASB), Copyright © 1960, 1962, 1963, 1968, 1971, 1972, 1973, 1975, 1977, 1995 by The Lockman Foundation. Used by permission. www.lockman.org.

Scripture quotations marked TPT are from The Passion Translation®. Copyright © 2017, 2018 by Passion & Fire Ministries, Inc. Used by permission. All rights reserved. ThePassionTranslation.com.

Scripture quotations marked MSG are taken from THE MESSAGE, copyright © 1993, 1994, 1995, 1996, 2000, 2001, 2002 by Eugene H. Peterson. Used by permission of NavPress. All rights reserved. Represented by Tyndale House Publishers, Inc.

Scripture quotations marked NKJV are taken from the New King James Version®. Copyright © 1982 by Thomas Nelson. Used by permission. All rights reserved.

ISBN: 978-1-949784-75-6
eISBN: 978-1-949784-76-3

Library of Congress Number: 2021909639

Cover Design: Deryn Pieterse
Cover Image: Peter Olexa

Printed in the United States of America

To all those confused by their current or past suffering or terminal diagnosis. Life is hard and full of disparities between those who have and have not experienced challenges, chronic illnesses, tragedies, or loss. God really is with you and isn't punishing you, like some well-meaning but religiously confused people say. Wit and I dedicate her story to those often shamed by uber-religious people who have all the answers but little wisdom. Wit's story defends both God and the one suffering by revealing what we really mean when we say faith. Faith doesn't help you get what you want; faith is what you need when you don't get what you want.

CONTENTS

INTRODUCTION

When you grieve the loss of an older person, you grieve the loss of yesterdays. When you lose a child, you grieve the loss of tomorrows. And when you grieve the loss of the God you thought you knew, the suffering is intensified.

When I lost my twenty-seven-year-old daughter, Whitney, to cancer, I began a long journey of grieving tomorrows. We believe in a miracle-working God who could heal our Wit, but we didn't get the miracle. My faith in God has been tested and my relationship with God has evolved over time.

Wit's life story is coated with fragrant joy, personal beauty, natural wittiness, and a kindheartedness toward all living things. She was courageous and had a knack for one-line zingers that made her unforgettable. She was both graceful and clumsy in an amusingly appealing way. She was quirky and intellectually brilliant with an air of "I don't care what people think of me"—even though she very much did. She taught me so much during her life, and I continue learning from her even today as I reflect on her life and her faith in an unchanging God.

Wit inspired thousands through her music to connect to the God they could not see. Through her songs, journals, and personal experiences, you will come to understand her faith in God—even during suffering. Wit's story will make you smile, think, and cry; and it will help you feel more in touch with your own journey. There is a way for your faith to make the voyage through personal pain—and even your disappointment with God. I know because I've lived through it, and in this book, I hope to share my journey with you.

This theologian, intellectual, and pastor did not need a faith as strong as Wit's until I became a traumatized and grieving dad. This book is a blended story—Whitney's and mine—of how we came to know the God of mystery better through suffering. These pages share the remarkable and resilient faith of a young woman who did not allow a terminal diagnosis to define what life she had left or diminish her worship of and love for God.

PART I

NOT GETTING
THE MIRACLE

CHAPTER 1

LIGHT UP

It is in silence, and not in commotion, in solitude and not in crowds that God best likes to reveal Himself most intimately to men.[1]

—Thomas Merton

Wit was five years old and could hardly see out of the windows of the tan minivan. We were just arriving for our vacation in the Blue Ridge Mountains and headed to the local diner for a meal. Over the last hour of our trip Brayden, my oldest child, had spotted several deer. Though he called out these sightings, Wit missed each one. She brought a little yellow box Kodak camera to take pictures of any animals; she was especially upset about missing these sightings.

Suddenly, she announced, "God loves my brother more than me. Unless I see a deer tonight, I will know God doesn't love me."

I replied, "Wit, you can't ask God to drop a deer in front of our minivan."

My newly framed Master of Divinity degree gave me all the authority I needed. I told her that even if we didn't see a deer, God still loved her very much. I spent the whole dinner gently nudging her to see things my way. She was unrelenting. "Unless I see a deer on the way back to our cabin, I'll know God loves Brayden more than me."

I worked carefully with her young heart, talking about how nature makes its own decisions and animals roam the mountains to eat and are often wary of cars and people. I hate to admit, it never actually occurred to me to ask God for help. When we neared the cabin, I heard her yell from the back seat, "There's one!" I eased on the brakes, and we came to a stop four feet from what looked like a young doe. I was shocked. The small deer stood by the mailbox and stayed there as we parked. Wit unbuckled, walked over to the oversized van window, and started snapping pictures like crazy.

As we sat there, I explained that she should not expect an answer like this every time she prayed. I had just started to pull back onto the country road when she declared, "I must see baby rabbits on the side of the road, or this doesn't count!"

"You can't just ask for that," I said firmly. But within three van lengths, we saw an entire family of rabbits lined up shoulder to shoulder—including babies—feeding on the edge of that country road. She unbuckled again, and the shutter of the little yellow Kodak camera clicked repeatedly.

Even decades later, whenever I see a deer, I am reminded of that coming-to-faith moment—and I am reminded of God's presence in Wit's life. As Wit grew and matured, so did her faith. She was bold and unique, from the clothes she wore to the music she wrote to the rare, old-school personal virtues she carried. This poet, sister, daughter, wife, songwriter, musician was primarily a relentless worshiper of God.

Wit's passion and talent led her to become a worship pastor and write melodies of her own. She created atmospheres for people to enter God's presence; to see their own deer and baby rabbits, so to speak. Her voice was powerful, but her faith was even stronger.

Her talent, voice, passion, and faith are all present in her original songs on her first album, titled _Light Up_. No matter what season she was in, she trusted in God and His love for her. Ever since that faith-shaping moment in the tan minivan, Wit has been teaching me about faith in a mysterious and loving God.

Whitney Vesterfelt

_____

The usually happy, perky voice quivered with fear and uncertainty over the phone. "It's called Hodgkin's Lymphoma," Wit said.

I recognized her voice but not the words. Cancer names were like a foreign language to our family; they are not now. She and her husband, Allen, were living in Nashville when she called with the final diagnosis. The muffled sounds of people talking and everyday life carrying on in the background seemed odd and out of place—Wit's world and mine had just been silenced by her report. Wit would begin treatments within the month; she was only twenty-three.

People often tried to comfort us by saying this was the "good" kind of cancer. We heard it was beatable, so we felt optimistic. Even so, Wit worked hard to conceal from her mother, brother, and me the difficulty of her treatments. Having been devoted to only putting good things in her body since she was a very little girl, overcoming the internal hurdle of what those treatments did to her body was difficult for her every single time. If you know someone who has submitted to treatments, you know there's a whole language around it.

At first the language medical staff and doctors used sounded like a professional boxing match. Everything comes in what they called "rounds." Wit's first "round" of treatment lasted six months. However, just before that "first round" of poison was pumped into her body, they had to install a port in her upper chest cavity. The port is designed to carry toxic medicine straight into the bloodstream. Wit's cancer was a cancer of the blood, so there is no way to remove this type of cancer through surgery.

Right after the opening bell of this fight—days into her first round of treatments—Wit got an infection and became septic. She was hospitalized for ten days, and the doctors said she narrowly escaped death; they estimated by about four hours. Even a minor delay could have ended her journey right there.

As round one ended with six months and hair loss, a scan revealed a spec of cancer doctors referred to as a "light-up." This term comes up often for people diagnosed with Hodgkin's Lymphoma. Essentially, the scans used liquid substances called *radionuclides* or *tracers*. If cancer was present, the tumor or area affected would "light up" to indicate increased cell activity. So, they said, "We still see some light-up. We will have to move to round two."

Wit had ten rounds of chemotherapies and treatments. Ten. Like a boxing match with two evenly matched opponents squaring off. Each round had a different kind of challenge: some had hair loss; some had other horrible side effects. Just like in boxing, it was a match decided by the judges, and since we felt we knew the ultimate Judge, we thought she would be declared the winner. But the Judge ruled against us.

The medical community also use the language of stages. It's more like a mixed martial arts (MMA) fight, often referred to as caged fighting. Unlike boxing, with its defined rules and etiquette, this is a full contact combat based on various martial arts techniques from around the world. Wit's MMA fight was otherworldly and it was absolutely full contact. Cancer of any kind, but especially cancer of the blood, never fights fair.

It was a spiritual, mental, physical, emotional, and vocational battle. She battled mentally with thoughts of: *Should I get treatment at all? Why not just trust God and go off all these treatments and demonstrate complete faith?* After year three and ten rounds of treatment behind her with nothing to show for it, the doctors released her to go it on her own. They had no further hope or options, and Wit embraced that as a relief.

Early in the cancer journey, Wit asked her husband to place a chair next to her bed so that if Jesus came to heal her during the night, He could sit and stay awhile. She took communion hundreds of times, increased spiritual exercises, and deepened her contemplative worship life, but the kind of visitation we all prayed for never happened. The chair in her room remained empty all four years.

Like Wit's bold ultimatum to see a deer, we believed fervently that God would heal her—that it was in His very nature to heal her. No amount of grit, positive talk, or sincere prayer and belief could stop the inevitable. Only God could have stopped it. He didn't.

Six months before the Covid-19 pandemic was made public, August 6, 2019, at 3:33 in the morning she took her last breath.

———————

My family and I decided that Wit's naming her album *Light Up* could not be a coincidence. Until you've experienced a major health issue or walked with a family member or friend through the medical system, it's tough to unpack the range of emotions you experience. The highs and lows of health and healing, the good news and the bad, and the anxiety waiting for the phone to ring—it is all excruciating.

With even the medical terminology constantly reminding us of Wit's resiliency and presence, we had hope. God had gone in front of us to prepare us all for the struggle and victorious outcome that would be ours. But because of our hope and our refusal to believe God would allow us to become another cancer-death statistic, we failed to see that God might be using her songs to send an eternal message instead.

There are six songs on Wit's album, and "Light Up" stands in stark contrast to the other songs. Although it shows her versatility as an artist and songwriter, it surprises the listener with a gritty and edgy electric guitar opening, played by Wit's husband. She was avant-garde in all she did, so it shouldn't have surprised me, but I couldn't believe she selected it as the title track. Looking back over her four-year battle, I think she picked the title track unknowingly, because it ended up as the phrase she heard repeated year after year. "Yes, Wit, we still see light-up."

These lyrics became not just the words of her title track but also the soundtrack we would live by:

> *My faith my faith's increasing, believing my God will see me through*
> *My feet my feet are planted, on Christ alone I'm standing, my God won't let me go*
> *We can't contain it, we won't restrain it, nothing can silence the sound*
> *Our hearts are beating, ever increasing, making your praises loud*
> *You are strong and mighty, Full of grace and mercy*
> *Your love shines within us, So we will live in your light*
> *Revive, Revive the nations, till all creation's singing*
> *Our God Our God makes all things new*
> *Ignite, ignite our hearts God, with the great holy fire*
> *Our God, Our God won't relent*
> *Light up light up light up, light up*
> *The whole world God let your kingdom come*
> *Light up light up light up, light up*
> *The whole world God let your kingdom come*

During the four years post-diagnosis, her scans continued to show activity, while God seemingly did not. Every light-up was a letdown. The way the cancer ravaged her body—especially in those last few months—still haunts our family. The images are too horrific to put in writing, but we were all traumatized by the experience. We still struggle to believe God was helping her at all then.

The unbearable weight of every decision to do another round of chemo and sign up for more suffering was excruciating to say the least. It was painful to seek cure after cure, all the while believing there would be a miracle somewhere in Wit's story. Yet hopes on this side of eternity went unmet.

Years of fervent prayer and intercession, standing in faith, and believing with great passion ended. Hopes and prayers silenced, absorbed into the God who remained quiet in her pain and passing. Silenced were the misinterpreted dreams of people who imagined her healed on this earth. Silenced were the prophetic predictions of healings that never came. We thank God for people who cared enough to take the risk and believe with us for a miracle and are strengthened by that love to this day. They all carry pain and grief in their hearts too.

Trying to explain the unexplainable and describe the indescribable is impossible without using metaphors. Facing something you've never faced before means you will need an idea or concept with deeper meanings to communicate your sense of what's happening. This fight (that's a metaphor) to explain with clarity a mystery is the challenge when it comes to shattered beliefs about the God you thought you knew. The struggle to communicate while in your deepest pain is exhausting because you know that few will truly understand. Finding the right metaphor allows rest for the heart and room to explore the new territory and realities that you're learning about God, yourself, and what comes next.

Silence from God when you need Him most feels cold and out of character for the God we are told about in church—the God I thought I knew. But in reality, at least part of that isn't true. It does feel cold when God chooses to remain silent, but it's only a sign you are in the winter season. The Bible says that God "made both summer and winter."[2] He is the God of every season. In the silence, He removes the awareness of His presence intentionally; it's one of the great mysteries church leaders have talked about for centuries. Throughout church history, priests, monks, nuns, ordinary Christ-followers have all written about the "dark" night of the soul, a time when the silence makes it feel like God has forsaken you.

Silence will always feel like a winter season to me. When you see fruit on a tree in the early summer, all seems to be fine, beautiful, and right. But winter exposes a tree for what it is—it is bare, and all its flaws and bumps are visible to the world. Wit's favorite time of year was the overlap of fall and winter: the trees were authentic, bare, and honest in appearance. That shift in seasons marked a transition for all of nature—from green leaves and fruit to completely barren. Although the winter tree appears to be dead, it is actually undergoing a process called dormancy that will only strengthen the tree and preserve it. Winter forces the tree to pull from inside itself to survive the brutal weather. The leaves fall and deformities are exposed. The tree has never been more alive because each winter brings more endurance—as the seasons pass, the tree grows stronger. Like the trees, Wit stayed strong, rooted, and honest during the winter season of her life. In her dark night of the soul, she continued to be a light. Like the tree she was in transition—in her final winter, but not dead—only undergoing a process that would make her flourish forever.

God's silence is like a frigid winter, and there's no way to know how long it will last. That's the part I personally was unprepared for, even though my vocation was to help people walk through their pain and loss. I must admit now that I did not understand the depth of internal pain, suffering, and trauma these families experienced. How could I?

Seminary can't give you empathy and experience, and Jesus' suffering—
the truth that we are told we will suffer too (see 1 Pet. 2:21)—is still just
a concept until you end up suffering.

Paradoxically, the one thing you're never exposed to in most
churches is silence. Some like their spirituality noisy and full of activity,
like spiritual springs and summers all the time. But the spiritual winters
are more ominous and quieter, silent even, and always bitterly cold. Yet
I have found that God's silence is an invitation to a spiritual doorway to
perseverance and powerlessness—it is the way of the cross. His silence
kills the deepest roots of self-love and forces a rebirthing of one's faith
in the God you cannot see. There are no directional signs on the road
of silence to even show you if you're heading in the right direction, but
you wake up each morning trusting that you'll figure it out today. There
are no mile markers to indicate how far you must still travel, only an
inner sense that this is the path you are supposed to walk. The way of
the cross is to walk in a powerless place; it will never be easy or comfortable or popular.

The God I expected to show up did not. At the very least, that meant
some of what I learned in church and seminary just was not true for
everyone. The picture of God that I had drawn in my head is not the
same as the God I have come to know after Wit's death. He is but He
isn't. You see, I thought I knew Him—and I did, just not very well. What
happened to me and my family is a forced expansion of understanding
how God relates to our everyday troubles. But when that forced expansion happens, one becomes disoriented. Everything seems different
because it is different.

This winter season has led to a fuller understanding of the God of
suffering and God of mystery. As a middle-class American who hadn't
needed much in the way of miracles, God's silence amid my family's
suffering began deconstructing the image of God I'd built—an image of
prosperity, health, and protection from pain. I began reading the Bible

in a different way. Verses that I'd read hundreds of times took on a new meaning. Particularly verses like this one:

> *He was despised and rejected by mankind, a man of suffering, and familiar with pain. Like one from whom people hide their faces he was despised, and we held him in low esteem.*[3]

Suffering—deep, unspeakable suffering—disfigures you, changes you, and reshapes you. It makes you unrecognizable to others and sometimes even to yourself. Many of the religious people in Jesus' time didn't recognize Him as the Messiah. Most of them had centered their lives around the expectation of having the great military liberator free them from their current oppression and discomfort.

The idea that God would come to Earth and suffer—for us—and become intimately familiar with pain doesn't line up with most people's religious expectations today either. Just like in the first century, the devout have developed false expectations. We expect a God who will show up, protest our personal pain, and fix the situation. I actually used this passage in Isaiah in my prayers and protests against Wit's disease. But a careful reading in context helps us see that these verses were given to show how the God who loved her so much intimately and uniquely understood her pain; He walked the path just in front of her.

He was a man of suffering and familiar with pain. Jesus was tested and tempted in every way that we are.[4] He isn't disconnected from our reality, emotions, and hardships—He has lived through it. He has experienced God's perceived silence in suffering. He invites us into suffering for His sake, just like His disciples and followers.

Before Jesus was tried and sentenced to torture and death, He was aware of His fate and the suffering He would face. He knew His purpose, but knowing didn't make it any easier. Just before He was arrested, tried, and crucified, He went to a garden to ask God to remove the burden of suffering from Him: "My Father, if it is possible, may this cup be taken from me. Yet not as I will, but as you will."[5] While it is difficult for us to feel what Jesus felt as He prayed that "agonizing prayer," we also see that the Father did not take the cup from Him. Jesus was enveloped in silence just like Wit was, like I am.

This silence and inaction from God in the heavens when the hearts here on Earth are so full of agony feels insensitive at best and uncaring at worst. And yet, deeply spiritual people, like Wit, are those who wake up early in this world. Over time, they reveal more to us about the love of God and our eternal lives in and with Him forever. Believing all the right doctrines on healing and or the supernatural are much less important than loving God "with all your heart and with all your soul and with all your mind."[6]

Truthfully, it wasn't God's fault Wit got cancer. That's just not God's nature. The truth is that God submitted Himself to the human predicament by standing in full solidarity with us in our suffering. We see in the crucifixion that God may seem silent and inactive in our lives currently, but in other ways He has already spoken, in that He came to identify fully with the human condition. At dinner with His disciples before His crucifixion, Jesus tore a piece of bread and told them, "This is my body broken for you."[7] Even near the end of John 6, we see Him saying that His body is for their consumption. This is God Himself becoming food for us, manna in our own wilderness of suffering. His life was offered up for Wit, for you, and for me. The physical, wounded body of Christ—God the Son—was offered to us.

I don't know how I had missed this reality that life—and all our lives—has a crucifixion pattern to it. Jesus embodied for us the tension of living in a broken world. I learned this mystery from my own daughter as she lived in this place of tension. Wit took care of her body, stewarded her body, and, in the end, offered it back to God as worship, just as

Scripture tells us to do.[8] In suffering for four years down in the trenches of chemotherapy—even though there was silence—the eternal God and final judge gave permission for Wit to suffer.

Wit embodied worship as she fought the cancer and all throughout her winter season. Worship was deeper and more central to her life than even her diseased blood! This too is still a mystery for me. Unfortunately, maybe even irreverently, we've reshaped the woundedness, suffering, and resurrection of Jesus to fit our own messages of "rising above," using it to perpetuate the idea that we will never suffer or experience bad things. It's a message that never worked in some parts of the world where persecution and poverty ruled the day. The reason it can't work is because we are His body to be broken for this world as the "embodying" of His presence among the people of this world.

Annie Dillard critiques the American church in her book *Teaching a Stone to Talk*:

> *Why do people in churches seem like cheerful, brainless tourists on a packaged tour of the Absolute? . . . On the whole, I do not find Christians, outside the catacombs, sufficiently sensible of the conditions. Does anyone have the foggiest idea what sort of power we so blithely invoke? Or, as I suspect, does no one believe a word of it? The churches are children playing on the floor with their chemistry sets, mixing up a batch of TNT to kill a Sunday morning. It is madness to wear ladies' straw hats and velvet hats to church; we should all be wearing crash helmets. Ushers should issue life preservers and signal flares; they should lash us to our pews. For the sleeping god may wake some day and take offense, or the waking god may draw us out to where we can never return.*[9]

The domesticated God many Americans talk about is not God, or at the very least is a diluted version full of the American dream, positive thinking, and a good work ethic but of very little help when facing a diagnosis like Wit's. My tradition, though incredibly sincere, often misses the target with shallow positive messages on a Sunday. We all need more realism and authenticity when it comes to facing the worst things in this life.

American spiritual triumphalism—the idea that you can command something to happen and for it to happen at will—is not only a lie but has also tainted true spiritual victory and caused many to abandon their faith altogether. This kind of spirituality—and I use that word loosely here—creates Hollywood-like heroes who are likable, can tuck their shirt in, run their church like a well-oiled machine, and inspire us to call upon the miracle-working God in our suffering. However, I have forever lost touch with the God who feels like an insulated blanket protecting me from a chilly world. No, I feel more like a soldier in a foreign country trying to survive the winter, crouched behind a rock, soaked with holes in my wet gloves, eating pork beans out of a can. You will feel disappointed and let down by God because His purposes and plans may not include keeping you happy, or healthy, or whole. Although it's hard to swallow, God actually wants broken and humble people, and those attributes won't come into your life without challenge, trouble, and suffering.

Silence deconstructs shallow belief systems and worldviews and can lead one to an unshakable foundation that can withstand "all" the storms of life. Winters are more brutal in the north than the south and their duration is much longer. Maybe some believers get to live a pretty comfortable suburban Christianity, like mild winters in the spiritual south. And perhaps some of us have to live in spiritual places where even the basics of life, faith, and belief come through a frigid fight to survive long winters when God seems very far from our struggle. Wit's passing crushed our insulated happy family—living in the spiritual south—who only spoke joyfully of the blessings in this life. Following her death, we do not start each day from joy but rather profound sadness. To this day, we have to fight to get into joy, and we don't make it every day. Yet we are coming to believe that God's silence is also a message to be considered.

There are moments in your life that change you forever. They initiate suffering that outstrips human learning, where only heavy sighs or guttural grunts reveal your pain. The harshness of the winter of the soul is much too frigid for ordinary devotion. Since we are a family of faith, it seems to me that our suffering is exacerbated. The medical community tried to prepare her and us for the ultimate outcome, and we always understood what science was saying. Yet because of our deep belief in God's nature as a loving Father, we said to ourselves, "But God!" For us, Wit's suffering and death have turned out to be life-altering and confusing in terms of the God we thought we knew. Those kinds of moments will ultimately challenge how you feel about God, your view of the way the universe works, your understanding of yourself, and even His oversight of your life. Here's an excerpt of a poem I wrote the first winter without Wit.

> Bounty and blessing fade as winter falls.
> The winter season, with its icy nights and frigid ground,
> when all goes dark and death does what it does,
> the God of the seasons mysteriously quiet and still.

I have a much deeper appreciation for silence now: outside the view of religious services—humbled and reverent silence is deeply moving, powerful, and holy. Jesus is the ultimate example of and reason for faith: clinging to the God you love even when suffering comes and He is silent. Silence doesn't mean He's not there. Faith is continuing to look for deer, even when you haven't seen one for miles. Faith is continuing to pray for a miracle, even when scans continue to light up. Faith is continuing to remember the fruit of summer, even as the snow falls.

––––––––––

When Wit died, we realized we had never really contemplated that possibility. As naïve and gloomy as that may sound, we had never allowed ourselves to go there in our minds or with our mouths. The general thought was that we wanted to stay hopeful; we came to believe that being full of faith meant you stayed positive in your declarations. While that may be great for business and perhaps even true for some people, my experience tells me winter comes to most—if not all—of us. To stand in the middle of a blizzard while talking positive about sunshine and denying the storm may not produce any warmth in the frigid temperatures of God's silence and your suffering.

The way you think about God in your life should never be reduced to just being positive about what you are going through. No amount of human effort or positive talk can accelerate a season of suffering and bring it to an end. When it's winter, it's winter! It's best to fully accept the season you're in with humility and ask for strength to endure. Submit yourself peacefully to the winter seasons of your life, bear your sufferings, and receive any hints of joy as a promise of spring. Silence from God during your suffering is an invitation into solidarity with other believers from every century past and people from around the world. And it ultimately leads to knowing God in new ways and developing a deeper, stronger relationship with Him.

One thing that writing and journaling have done for me is help me see that God's communications in the past are often relevant to my situational silence in this present moment. Some might say God's silence is a test, and the teacher always stays silent during a test. But that metaphor, like most other spiritual metaphors, breaks down if it's taken literally—it would mean God let my daughter die to test me, that her life was somehow less than mine. Or that she was a tool to get a point across to me. Do you see the absurdity in that kind of thinking? In silence, there are no easy answers and sometimes only mystery. But there is a God who has communicated love in the past and will again in my future.

Wit's husband of eight years gave me and my wife Wit's journals and all of her published music as we helped pack up her things and sell their home after her passing. The journals were a priceless gift for which I'll be eternally grateful. One of the first journals I opened had Wit's rewrite of John 10. It's the passage where Jesus says we are His sheep and He is our shepherd. Wit journaled, "He calls His own sheep by name and leads them out. When He has brought them outside, He goes on ahead of them. The sheep follow His voice. They won't follow a stranger because they don't recognize the voice of a stranger." Immediately following that rewrite, she penned, "I set my eyes on you and not on sickness, not even the solution. Eyes on you, listening for the voice I know so well. Ready to follow. I will follow where it leads, surrendered, and unafraid." Then she wrote lyrics to a song that was not fully finished called "The Voice of God." Here's one of my favorite lines: "The voice of God sounds like peace, sounds like love, sounds like grace … celebrate when He speaks."

In going through Wit's journals, I saw three recurring principles. These three principles defined Wit's life and her journals gave me evidence of their importance in coping with God's silence during an illness or loss of a dream: wisdom, integrity, tenacity. W.I.T. What set Wit and her faith apart was the presence of these three traits. Her wisdom, integrity, and tenacity helped her through silence, winter, light-ups, and letdowns.

Sitting on the floor, legs folded and head in my hands, a few weeks after Wit had passed, I wrote out my prayers. I was devastated and personally shattered, as all my hopes and dreams for our family were gone. My daughter would not get to have children of her own—children she desperately wanted. She would never lead us in worship again. How does one mourn the unknown loss of never holding your future grand-kids? The sight of empty benches at the large handcrafted dining table aches daily, and on holidays it is nearly unbearable.

While down on the floor with no audible prayer possible, I wrote one out. I prayed for wisdom so that I could worship God like Wit would want me to. I prayed for integrity of heart, that I would be honest with God and others about the God who had let me down. I prayed for the tenacity not to abandon my faith and to show courage like she did every day as she battled her disease. In those moments on the floor of a hotel room, I knew I had been given a gift: her template to help with my pain. I had found my path. It's the path this book will use to guide you. Let's continue to walk with Wit together in the chapters ahead and listen for the path you are to take in your living and in your dying. I pray that her wisdom, integrity, and tenacity through her suffering will encourage you in your faith like it's encouraged me.

WISDOM MOMENT

Grab your journal and form a one-sentence prayer from one of the following statements.

God, I believe You may have been communicating with me through . . .

God, in this silent winter season I am listening for . . .

God, in this moment, help me to come close to (name of friend) who is enduring a winter.

INTEGRITY MOMENT

Write out a confession about your relationship with God. Include any frustration with God's silence on something or disappointment with Him that you've never admitted. Don't hold anything back.

TENACITY MOMENT

Plan a quiet time for you and God to sit together in silence. Try to calm your mind and be fully present. Maybe plan on ten minutes, grab a mug of hot tea or coffee, and keep your journal open. Think deeply about how you currently view your situation. Record any thoughts that seem to offer the most strength and hope.

CHAPTER 2

HERE COMES THE SON

Musicians work with time as one note follows another note, the way tock follows tick . . . Music helps us to "keep time" . . . as a stream that every once in a while slows down and becomes transparent enough for us to see down to the streambed . . . past, present, and future are so caught up in a single moment that we catch a glimpse of the mystery that, at its deepest place, time is timeless.[10]

—Frederick Buechner

Wit's story nearly ended before it began. The doctor and his team filled the room. I sat the heavy video camera on the sterile tile floor—the birth of our second child was not going well. The medical team worked with deliberate movements; her skin was completely dark blue or black. She was not breathing. They all seemed calm at first, but as their intensity picked up, so did our heart rates.

The nurse kept flipping Whitney, that's the name we had picked out, back and forth from her back to her stomach. The doctor stepped in forcefully and took her—the next sixty seconds were an eternity. My feet were frozen to the floor. Darla's view was blocked, but her eyes showed a growing panic as they scanned the room. Then we heard that sweet voice for the first time. She was breathing, and we could too. Her skin flushed with pinky tones, and all would be fine for twenty-three more years.

The big clock showed two hours and nineteen minutes; it was after midnight on May 24, 1992. Followed by my parents, Brayden walked in six hours later with a playful smile as he saw his sister for the first time. He held flowers for Mom in one hand and a tiny stuffed animal for sis in the other. He was talkative and tender as we squeezed him in between Mom and the bed's side rail. They both held little Whitney for the first time on his lap. He told Wit about all the things they would do together.

On Wit's first night home after being born, I prayed the same prayer I had prayed over her brother. I asked God to help me know how to pray over her life each evening when we tucked her in for bed. By the end of that week, I had the prayer to pray. I would touch her soft little head every night and say, "God, I pray that You will put a song in her heart." God did answer that prayer. Whitney always loved music and singing— from the lullabies her mom and I sang to her when she was young, to the times in her teens when we would listen to the Cranberries on our way to run errands, to her leading worship and writing songs as a young adult. She once told me, "Music has the power to make someone feel a quiet disposition that compels a listen. It's, by nature, non-threatening. Sometimes this is the preferred way to communicate. The beauty in it has a way of disarming others. Music is just one of the expressions of worship. My personal preference." She always had a song in her heart.

Her album, *Light Up*, showcases her passion and talent for music as well as her deep, enduring faith. The first song declares that God's love encompasses the human experience, and now we know that includes suffering and cancer. What we experience in the daytime may not be what we experience at night. Wit wrote to her future self just six months before the diagnosis: "You are with me, You are here." The song "Sunrise" is a declaration of God's caring oversight. The veiled reference to the children of Israel passing through the wilderness is obvious to a person raised in church. The message is that God was with them in the blistering heat of the day by cloud and in the colder temperatures at night by fire. He is the God of the daytime, and He is the God of the night. Solar spirituality, when the good things going on in your life warm the face and pull a smile, is much easier to journey toward God than a lunar spirituality, where a quarter moon sky provides only a small glimmer of hope.

> *Like the coolness of the shade, the warmth of the sun*
> *melody of a song, like returning home*
> *You are with me, You are near*
> *and I'm so glad to sing*
> *Oh, here we go*
> *Oh, here we go*
> *Like sunrise to sunset*
> *your love covers me like a*
> *cloud by the day or the stars at night*
> *Like a whisper in the night, or something that's unseen*
> *a shelter from the storm, a cloud's covering, you are with me*
> *you are here, and I'm so glad to sing*
> *I can testify that the Lord is good,*
> *yes the Lord is good all the time*
> *From sunrise to sunset your love covers me like a cloud by the*
> *day or the stars at night*
> *Yea, I can testify that the Lord is good,*
> *yes the Lord is good all the time*

Wit was a songbird even in the nighttime of her life, and God watched over her just like He watches over the birds that fly around us in the day and at night too.

_____

Wit's last appearance leading worship on a Sunday morning was eleven months before she died. That day the fluid in her body had reached such a stage that both of her lungs collapsed under their pressure. She sang until she couldn't because it was her way of bringing out the beauty of the world and of God—and she did both so well. Singing was her way of bringing others into a deeper relationship with and understanding of the God she served, and I'm still learning from her songs today. The song God put in her heart, the song of her life, was far beyond what I could've hoped or imagined. I wanted her song to be longer, I prayed that it would be longer, but I was let down. Little did I know when I was praying for God to put a song in her heart, I was also praying for my future self, that I would have as a lasting strength the lyrics and melodies God knew I would need to hear.

Four years we pursued God and prayed with sincerity—her mom leading all day and night prayer vigils. Brayden and his wife, Heather, placing hands on her and praying with intensity of heart. Her husband taking communion with her. Grandparents and family members praying for help. Devout people of notoriety you might know praying to the God of heaven, and yet nothing changed. Her lead doctor was very engaged in the prayer effort to see God do something extraordinary. Today, my heart is full of gratitude as I look back and remember how dear friends stood in faith with us, not to mention a church that prayed for her night and day. Their steadfastness with us to seek God for a miracle in our suffering is now priceless. Yet, there was no miracle, only the absence of one.

No one was able to protect or save Wit from her cancer, not even her dad. She fought so bravely over those four years. Much of her journey is documented through her Instagram posts and YouTube videos that are still accessible. Whitney loved God and wasn't afraid to show it publicly. But she, like us, came to see that we do serve a God who will sometimes "let us down." He did not save her from the cancer or the ending we all denied with our mouths in unwavering faith. We all endured with trust, worship, and confidence in God's ability to deliver a breakthrough. And even though He had the ability to do it, and some testify that He has done it for them, the Way-maker never came through for us. The hard truth is that sometimes God does not give you what you ask for, no matter how sincerely you ask.

We felt mortality with every scan; setback after setback brought relentless disappointments. She had one of the best doctors, ten rounds of treatments, hair loss several times, and the new innovative immunotherapy that you hear about on the news—and yet nothing could stop the scans from lighting up with cancer. But the elephant in the room was that we all knew God could stop it! Wit had decided, and the whole family agreed, that we should go after her healing, blending the expertise of science with passionate, sincere prayer. Ironically, this faith, trust, and love for God exponentially increased our suffering because we knew God could stop the cancer and the pain, and we watched as He did not. We never considered the "what if God doesn't come through" outcome. Part of our deep grief and part of the reason Wit's loss is still so hard to accept is that, even though we believed God could do a miracle, He didn't. I was raised in a tradition and spent several hundred thousand dollars training for a vocation whose foundation is predicated on a miraculous God. I taught others that God would "make a way where there seems to be no way" but rarely mentioned to them the other possibility that He also might not. My platform of promise upon which I stood sunk into a puddle of tears as God did not make a way in this life.

The root word for "vocation" comes from *vocare* in the Latin, which means *to call* and is closely related to the Latin word *vox*, which means *voice*.[11] You see, for decades I used my voice to tell people God would work a miracle, and I would pray with them to that end. But when they didn't get a miracle, I had nothing to say to them. I do now. In fact, I have more in common with those who don't get a miracle than those who do. Like a spiritual father who has now endured some things he did not know before, I can use my voice and say to those diagnosed with terminal diseases or those enduring the grief years after everyone else has moved on, "I understand. I know."

One can get training on how to teach the Bible or be a pastor, to do this thing or that. But there isn't a class in seminary that can teach empathy, compassion, or identifying with people who suffer. It's one of those things one must learn through experience. However, I have learned that using our voices to empathize and express compassion is an equally important use of our voice as teaching the Bible. I want to use my vocation and voice to highlight the ministry of Jesus, as God submitted Himself to the cycle of pain that is the human condition. The cross of Jesus is far more important than Sunday-morning Christians can fathom. The contradiction of God having to suffer and experience the human condition speaks loudly then to the resurrection that changed Wit's future and mine. It's not that suffering "earns" anything, but rather suffering is the voice we use to call attention to God's loving kindness in the world. Wit, right in front of our eyes, resolved the contradiction by being the visible compassion of Jesus among us.

Wit's battle with cancer was a slow-motion tragedy that no one could stop, and God—the only One who could have stopped it—didn't. The spiritual disappointment I feel reaches to my core; I believe it is the greater part of my pain. Not only were thousands of people around the world praying for Wit, but her church and family were also interceding as Wit led thousands to worship this King we were counting on to defeat death. The God of victory, breakthrough, miracle worker, way maker, light in the darkness did not rescue or heal my daughter. Hundreds of positive proclamations and prophetic words and promises came through well-meaning people but nothing they shared came to pass. Of course, we should pray and ask—someone might even receive a physical miracle while reading Wit's story. But I also know that many will receive even deeper healings in their minds and hearts, which are just as miraculous as ones in the body.

It isn't our level of faith that determines our worthiness of miracles, and being Christ-followers doesn't excuse us from suffering—just ask His disciples. All eleven disciples suffered horribly and perished. This was after receiving the empowerment of the Sprit we see in Acts 2. Paul also suffered horribly as he embodied the message of Jesus all over the ancient world. As Jesus told the disciples in Matthew 10:39, "Whoever finds their life will lose it, and whoever loses their life for my sake will find it."[12] How did I ever get it in my mind that somehow Paul, the disciples, and many devout women and men were off base or lacking faith, which resulted in their suffering? And how did I come to believe my family was exempt from the assignment to vocalize death and resurrection in our own story? Rather than using Jesus to escape the suffering all around me in the world, I am a true disciple if I lose my life or what I expected in this life and embody the grief I am called to bear, showing resurrection to the world.

————————

About a year after Wit had passed, my wife, Darla, shared a Sunday message about John the Baptist, who found himself on death row. John sent disciples to Jesus and asked, "Are you the One?"[13] Jesus sent back a reply saying, "Go back and report to John what you have seen and heard: The blind receive sight, the lame walk, those who have leprosy are cleansed, the deaf hear, the dead are raised."[14] We could paraphrase it to say, "Please tell my cousin John that I'm doing miracles: blind eyes are being opened and even the dead live. However, I'm not coming to save you, and your miraculous deliverance from prison isn't going to happen." To me, this sounds harsh if you're John the Baptist because he would likely have had expectations for a miracle. Jesus had done these things for others, so why not for a family member?

Darla quoted Jesus' words in Luke 7:23: "The blessing of heaven comes upon those who never lose their faith in me, no matter what happens!"[15] Jesus basically told John, "Don't lose your faith even though I'm not coming to help." Darla made the connection to those walking through trauma now. She encouraged them not to fall away because they weren't spared their trauma. Jesus was essentially saying, "Blessed are those who don't abandon their faith in me, when I don't deliver them from their circumstances." Jesus not rescuing John foreshadowed Jesus' death and God not rescuing Him from the fate of the cross. And it also foreshadows the responsibility we have as followers of Jesus to embrace times of personal suffering, like John the Baptist did in prison and Jesus did on the cross. It is, literally, a practical embodiment of your faith. Jesus not rescuing John means that He won't always rescue us. Sometimes our story turns out more like John the Baptist's than we would want.

These themes of unmet expectations are prevalent in the Gospels as people are disappointed with Jesus time and again. When His friend Lazarus was suffering and on the verge of death, Jesus came to the rescue—four days late. Jesus' delayed response disappointed Lazarus's grieving siblings, Mary and Martha. The time delay between when they reached out to Jesus and Lazarus's time of death forced Mary and Martha into a horrible grieving pain.

Time forces a suffering on the human condition in a way only suffering people know. Not only were Mary and Martha watching Lazarus finally expire, but they were also holding onto hope that their miracle-working Master might appear and save the day. I believe those unmet expectations crushed them and created deep personal anguish because their expectations of Jesus had fueled hope. Perhaps someone else, maybe even living in their same small town, was watching their own loved one suffer that very week, watching them die. And the experience of that pain would have been lessened by having no expectations of a miracle.

Even though Jesus was close friends with Mary and Martha, He failed to break His silence after hearing how sick Lazarus was. They knew He had shown up for others, but He would not show up for them. In other words, they didn't just suffer because they watched Lazarus grow sicker and sicker but because their souls were deeply pained by their unanswered pleas. Jesus eventually did show up and He resurrected Lazarus and grieved with the sisters; but just like with John the Baptist, the response of Jesus, His eternal plan and execution were far less about relieving Mary and Martha's suffering than one might hope.

Just after Jesus raised Lazarus, He rode into Jerusalem to the cheers and adoration of so many who believe they would finally be released from the daily political oppression by the Romans. And Jesus wept for them because what they wanted was immediate relief from their situation, yet He was at work creating something brand new—something outside the system of spirituality they had known previously.[16] They desired a God who would give them what they wanted, what they expected, but He had something much bigger in mind—a plan that when executed would leave many of those very same people cheering disappointed beyond measure.

To feel disappointed by Jesus, to be thrust into the deepest suffering, far beyond what you believe you can physically, emotionally, and spiritually handle, is exactly where Jesus' friends and followers were—and it's what my family experienced of Jesus as well. Jesus disappointed them because He didn't give them inside information or remove their pain. Even though He wept, removing their pain didn't seem to be the point. Something else, something eternal and utterly beyond their comprehension, was taking place.

Shortly after Jesus rode through town surrounded by cheers of people who expected Him to bring liberation, His body was ravaged and His prayer that the cup be taken from Him was not answered. Mark describes the setting of the crucifixion in this way: "At noon, darkness fell across the whole land until three o'clock. Then at three o'clock Jesus called out with a loud voice . . . 'My God, my God, why have you abandoned me?'"[17] Jesus the Christ feeling abandoned by the Father in that moment may have been an even greater suffering than the physical pain He endured. When He revealed that He didn't want to drink the bitter cup of suffering, we see that Jesus Himself felt far from God, but in doing so, He showed the full extent of His humanity and solidarity with us all.

The Bible reveals God's nature to us in the suffering Jesus. God Himself did not avoid suffering. Unfortunately, suffering is the predicament of the human condition. The reframing of how we view our loved ones' suffering and our own deep suffering helps us when we understand that suffering in this life is not our penalty for sin. In Ecclesiastes 3 Solomon noted, "There is a time for everything, and a season for every activity under heaven . . . a time to weep and a time to laugh, a time to mourn, and a time to dance."[18] How is it that we think that "a time to mourn" won't apply to us if we pray and believe? Even Jesus experienced suffering and mourning.

Untrained or unseasoned Sunday speakers often skip the suffering of Jesus on the cross and our responsibility to endure seasons of suffering. Part of Jesus' messaging to us was to show that anything is possible, like miracles. Yet for the most part, His own life was about being shamed and rejected by those around Him, especially the religious establishment. There is a danger of simplifying all of Jesus' earthly ministry to a single moment of redemption. That school of thought leads to a "Jesus suffered so that I don't have to" mentality. The One who walked in our skin and comes close enough to us to help us carry our sorrows told us things could get bad.[19] When we only view God as the God of miracles and not also the God of mystery, we are destined to be disappointed when we don't get our miracle.

Imagine what the disciples must have felt when the sky darkened as Jesus took His last breath. Their own inner darkness and turmoil were represented in the sky above. The Son was gone, His light extinguished. The disciples didn't have the advantage of knowing the end of the resurrection story and did not know each of them—except John—would die excruciating deaths just like their Master. What we now know—three days of darkness until Jesus returned and was resurrected fulfilling prophecies and bringing hope to the world—they saw as a disappointing and gut-wrenching loss of a friend.

You can see it, can't you? This is a template for those who follow in the footsteps of the God-man Jesus. In one way or another, suffering will come to your life. If you get diagnosed with something terrible, I pray you get a miracle. But at some point, your miracles will run out and your suffering will result in God's new creation in you personally. We often don't talk much about how few true miracles we see in the States— at least, not in the circles I run in. We hear them paraphrased generically from the stage sometimes, but for those experiencing something ominous and terminal, we don't have a miraculous cure rate to use as encouragement. However, when it's your loved one hanging in the balance, you want something more concrete to confirm it's possible for God to show up and deliver from cancer, Alzheimer's, or other scientifically untreatable diseases.

In your darkest hour, when it may feel as if God has let you down, just know that He hasn't—He never promised you a life free from suffering. Many of Jesus' most trusted followers suffered horribly. Through enduring suffering with faith, you embody the message of hope to the rest of us—it's what Wit did, what the disciples did, and what we are called to do. The pattern of crucifixion in our lives is: cross, resurrection, and new creation. It never ends at the cross, where the suffering happens. There is always more to the story. He is the God of miracles, the God of healing, the God of suffering, and the God of nearness—all of those are true and unfathomably uncontradictory.

Wit was raised to believe in the miraculous God and never thought she was going to die. But the words of a song she wrote two years before her death expose that foretelling part of her. She wrote about losing her soul inside her bones, long before the cancer had gone that deep. She wrote about a fighter with no fight and a stranger, cancer, taking control. Then she writes to herself, to me, and to you to travel on.

Even though many of her treatments left her in misery, she was relentless in her worship, work ethic, and song writing. We have the audio recordings to some of them yet unreleased. One of the last songs she was working on was called "Travel On." It's a song we played at her memorial service for several thousand people.

> *There's a lost soul within your bones,*
> *You're a fighter with no fight*
> *There's a stranger taking control,*
> *You're a dreamer with no dream*
> *Away, away, you go, From what was once your home*
> *To live a life that's not your own, Your time has come*
> *Your hope's not lost though your sight is gone*
> *You're so tired of cold and grey*
> *Still there's a fire that grows and grows*

Travel on, Don't look back from where you are
The future's right in front of you travel on
Oh your best days are ahead of you
Close your eyes, Dream of a better life
Though it's not, I know the sun is gonna shine

Although the stranger taking control was cancer, it would not extinguish her fire. Travel on, friend, even though the sun's not shining; it will somewhere down the line, even if it's in the place with no time. You can do this with God's help. Keep traveling. Whether your story is more like Wit's or John the Baptist's, you know that it's all okay. Blessed are those who believe in Jesus and travel on regardless of the circumstances. Wit says, "Your best days are in front of you," and most times, I've known her to be right.

I believe prayer is important. I believe God answers prayer. I believe in miracles. I believe most of the people who teach how to get an answer to prayer know very little about it. Answered prayer is mysterious at best. I think we need to be prepared for times in our lives when God doesn't answer our prayers. Pandemics have a way of correcting bad thinking when it comes to the universe and God. The God of the Bible is always with you in the suffering but, from what I've seen, rarely intervenes to stop it.

I have learned that most of God's engagement in our world is not through supernatural rescues, though we still pray and believe with those who need one. Wit's story is more about enduring a non-answer to prayer and not losing your faith. She modeled being with people in their sufferings before she was sick and ended up with a medical team that cared deeply for her all four years. God uses human hands quite a bit more than we can see at first glance. But several things are important to get right. It is God who heals, not a person. The sincerity, frequency, consistency, volume, number of people praying do not equate to getting

God to do what you want. Faith in your journey is not your way to getting what you want—faith is what carries you through when you don't get what you want.

My family and I have experienced this trouble more than ever in the past few years. If I could do only one thing differently in parenting my daughter, it would probably be to prepare her for the possibility that God might let her down and not answer her prayers. Orlando was the place we raised our kids, the land of make-believe. But life is not a theme park where magical things come to life. Your children will need a strong heart to handle the disappointments and rejections that will inevitably come to them, and as followers of Jesus, we have a responsibility to tell them the truth.

Wit seemed to understand this better than I did during her last few months with us. In a post on her Instagram she said, "Despite what some say, I don't believe there is a formula for healing. God is mysterious. Every day is a surrender and trust." She had the wisdom to trust God even in her disappointment, the integrity to believe in God when the sun was not shining, and the tenacity to daily surrender to Him and His plan. From Wit's perspective, the miracle represented in her story was not walking away from cancer but walking through cancer. We—all of us—must learn to come boldly to Him and find not healing and not a miracle, but grace. We find grace to help us when we need it most.

Wit's life and story have now become an invitation to be certain of God's love, even in our uncertainty of His action as a result of our prayer. God is here with us. We know it like the plop sound a Florida frog makes on a very still lake in the morning, just beyond your eyesight—God with us and among us but not doing anything inside the realm of our knowing. Wit lived her life each day with love front and center. It impacted all who knew her, and we pray it impacts you too.

———————

The nearly two-thousand-seat auditorium was packed to the edges with the presence of God. A young woman, seated in the rear of the auditorium, later testified to this. She told me she had never felt God this deeply and in that kind of way. She said, "It was like I felt my hands just float up into the sky." She released her worries and apprehensions and had a spiritual awakening, some kind of supernatural occurrence, as Wit sang. This kind of God moment had happened before, but if you ask anyone who sat under her worship leading, it was unconventionally distinctive. Maybe a bad note here or there and sometimes wryly so, but Wit's thing was simply to sing. This songbird for God would sing, knowing God would shine into dark places of people's pain.

One Sunday, in the middle of a worship song with everyone singing, Wit "goes off," as the musicians would lovingly call it, leading everyone to a place they'd never been before. It was rapturous. Whatever song the rest of us were singing at the time, the bird on stage suddenly swooped upward. She took us all to an unanticipated height of exultant joy by bursting into the 1969 version of "Here Comes the Sun" by the Beatles.

She stepped to the front of the stage, kicking off her flats, rocking back and forth with microphone in hand, one leg well in front of the other. This five-foot-three little powerhouse was in the zone. The balding stage of chemotherapy had started the familiar transitioning to short stubble, and it somehow made her worship leading visually powerful. Wit took us all somewhere in that moment. It was fun, awesome, and deeply moving. Yes, she did—in a sense—relocate the entire audience from 2,000 seats in Sunday church to 90,000 seats in Wembley Stadium. In that song, in that moment, Wit declared winter over and that the Son was coming.

WISDOM MOMENT

Name the season you are currently experiencing: spring, summer, fall, or winter. Describe the season, perhaps using a metaphor. Use as many adjectives as possible, like, "This feels like the most frigid winter I've ever experienced," or "I long for the spring season and the fresh rains to bring newness to my soul." At any time, you can pull back and gain some perspective about where you are in this season of your life. This exercise can help you find the wisdom from God to help you through.

INTEGRITY MOMENT

Find a private place and use your voice. Say something verbally to God related to what situations you may be facing. Wit wrote "Travel On" not long before she passed. Journal about how you feel about traveling on from where you are today.

TENACITY MOMENT

What will you do if God doesn't rescue you but allows you to go on suffering in this life? God is with you. Finish this sentence: *My suffering forces me to ask God . . .*

CHAPTER 3

UMBRELLAS WON'T HELP IN A HURRICANE

We keep thinking that we ourselves will be spared when disaster strikes—until it is too late.[20]

—Dietrich Bonhoeffer

"There's another hurricane coming, Dad," twelve-year-old Whitney announced. It was 2004, two years before the cell phone and the internet would find each other and the same year Facebook was founded. She was right; in fact, Florida would end up having four hurricanes in just six short weeks. Three of those hurricanes would affect our house, with one of them bringing significant damage. Things were so ridiculous that the media rebranded Florida for a short period of time from the "Sunshine State" to the "Plywood State." Charley, Frances, Ivan, and Jeanne were their names, and their sustained presence did nearly a billion dollars of damage in Polk County alone. The eye of three of these four storms passed over our house. Charley killed thirty-one people. He was the strongest hurricane to hit Florida since Andrew in 1992.

The six of us, four humans along with one shih tzu and one cairn terrier, would spend the night and next morning in our oversized laundry room. As a young married couple, Darla and I had lived in tornado alley near Oklahoma City for years. Severe winds and dangerous storms were not new to us. Tornadoes in the Midwest give little warning; sometimes a siren goes off and sometimes it doesn't. But whatever happens—and it can be catastrophic—it is generally over within minutes. Charley—and some of the other storms that year—felt like twenty-four-hour tornadoes with freight trains charging through your living room.

None of us—Darla, Brayden, Whitney, or me—inside the beautiful two-story model home in 2004 were prepared for the devastation and suffering soon heading our way. A diagnosis of any kind hits more like a tornado than a hurricane because there is rarely any warning. No medical solution or the best insurance coverage could save us from our loss. No amount of science, money, divine favor, clean eating, prayer and fasting, faith, quoting Scripture, daily communion, church attendance, declaring positive statements of health, worship songs, good works, or ten rounds of chemotherapy and immunotherapy could keep the storm from devastating our family.

Before Wit's diagnosis and subsequent years of prayer, treatment, and suffering, I was largely unscathed by the storms of life. Married for thirty years with two beautiful and healthy children, the biggest storms we faced were hurricanes and planting a church near Sea World with little support. Nothing soul-shaking. Nothing permanent. Nothing utterly defeating.

The false assumption, a subtle spiritual arrogance resided in my heart that even if someone in our family got sick, God would take care of it. God loved us too much to allow one of us to die. I felt very intimate and close to God before Wit's death. Even though God is very close after Wit's death, I believe it by faith, not because I feel it. And I don't mean the kind of feeling like you're going steady or engaged with God, but I mean that you're in a deep covenantal marriage with God, and He's permitted this in your relationship. For me back then, it was just unthinkable. Now I see it as a mystery.

I did not know then what I do now: unsuspecting beautiful families can be hit by tragedy, sorrow, and traumas of all kinds. Our story is ordinary and our grief shared by thousands. The greater dilemma and tension we faced was our misunderstanding of who we thought God was, as the years with small storms provided a false sense of security.

Storms hit people whether they are followers of Jesus or not. Shallow religious understandings allowed me to live unaware that a dark and dangerous world could hit our family. My false assumption was that even if a storm hit, God would make a way to preserve our family unit. I had constructed a safe reality filled with church attendance and misunderstood Bible verses taken to mean that God would keep my kids from suffering. All those things turned out to be inadequate umbrellas that collapsed in our cancer hurricane.

It's impossible to enter into the pain of people dealing with horrific events and keep your view of a God who rescues good families from bad trouble. You must come to grips with the fact God does not always rescue people from trouble. Sincere religious people, like those in Jesus' day, often create distance between the God they thought they knew and the devastating circumstances around them by believing someone in the family has allowed evil in the door. The distance is created by believing there is no way God would allow unspeakable traumas to happen to good families, and if He did, then He would certainly send a miracle to stop it. If He doesn't stop it, then they were unworthy recipients.

For those not familiar with the Bible, the Gospel of John chapter 9 exposes these myths that still live today in the Bible belt. Jesus healed a grown man who had been blind from birth. It created controversy and debate because certainty and boxed up answers are incompatible with how faith works. This passage represents a very sincere question from Jesus' disciples. Essentially, they wanted to know, "Rabbi, why was this man born blind? Was it because of his own sins or his parents' sin?"[21] To go slowly through the chapter and read the whole story is to see that those who proclaimed to know God best in the story act as if the man and the family themselves got what they deserved.

Frankly, it's one of the great myths or misbeliefs people have; even a pandemic did not change some people's minds. Some sincere but unbiblical people think that if someone is not wealthy, happy, or blessed, then God has not favored them. People often think that if you suffer, then you or someone in the family has done something to bring this upon yourself. Essentially this *quid pro quo* view of God means that the person's actions are really what's controlling God's activity or lack of it.

The false assumption here is that since this man was suffering then surely he deserved it or his parents were being punished. The question displays an arrogance in thinking all suffering can be explained and blamed on someone. This arrogance is often seen in religious circles to this day, a false assumption that mysterious and tragic events can and should be explained by humanity's failings. These subtle superstitions suggest that you either earn God's favor and protection through good behavior or, if you're afflicted, we all know you had it coming.

It's easy to understand in those times—not that far removed from Alexander the Great or the Roman Empire with Caesar—how people viewed God as a great ruler who issued edicts, blessings, and curses. They feared God like they would any great ruler. The sentiment of countless people in that day could be summed up like this: "God is the angry cosmic Father throwing down judgments." Jesus' ministry exposes this gross misrepresentation of the nature of God. Jesus told His disciples, "If you have seen Me, then you have certainly seen the Father, who is always bringing the little children to Himself and caring for those with the least power in society."[22] The disciples were still experiencing the whiplash between the smiting God they imagined and the merciful Christ they were building a relationship with. Through Jesus' teachings and healings, He constantly expanded people's understanding and view of the God they thought they knew.

I suspect the biggest challenge to a limited view of God is that when suffering shows up, we have to downsize God to explain Him and what we think we know about Him. I think that, at best, a shallow or convenient view of God in our day has generated something like factory churches. Replacing Alexander the Great and Caesar the Lord as our template for understanding God, we now view God through the lens of mass-produced factories of religious motivations and inspirations. We are formulaic in our approach, creating certainties and absolutes where they don't exist.

In that way, we have all witnessed a systemized downsizing of God, where it's even possible to hate people of other races or religion, or even because of their sexuality, all in the name of fighting for a particular and limited view of God. We have developed theologies, or views of God, that allow us to villainize those whose life experiences fail to confirm what we think we know about God. Can you see how that takes us right back to John 9?

Jesus' response to the question of the blind man's sin speaks so much to God's mystery and sovereignty. He said, "Neither this man nor his parents sinned . . . but this happened so that the works of God might be displayed in him."[23] Many well-intentioned people make the jump from contemporary English to assume God makes people blind or have cancer so He can use them to make Himself look grander! Again, this view is a false narrative to hold together one's need to explain God rather than assign it to the mystery category. Think about it this way: If God caused people to suffer—striking the fetus blind in this case—and Jesus healed

Him, are we not pitting Jesus in a reversal against His own Father? One thing is clear to me on this journey: There is great suffering in this world, and it is not placed upon us by a loving God. Rather, Jesus came into the world to walk in our shoes and lead the way for God to make all things new, both now and in the end.

After Wit passed, I determined that I would be truthful about what our family experienced; I could no longer double down on putting God in a box by declaring that His nature allowed us to predict how He would respond. I subconsciously believed, as I think many people do, that if your faith does not move God's hand to get a miracle, then you are being punished from the heavens. This is at best sad and unbiblical and at worst sinful or idolatrous. Those who believe in the miracle-working God, and I still do, must let go of thinking we know how to help people get a miracle or "declare a healing," because we can't. All we can do is humble ourselves and ask.

Church camps, conferences, seminaries, and some Sunday sermons provide a beautiful collection of what I like to call theological umbrellas. These understandings of God, prayer, the supernatural, and spiritual beliefs associated with Bible verses taken out of context lie in a box by the front door and are deployed when the storms of life come. They help us stay dry and warm within our chosen, limited understanding of God and safe from the elements of the world constantly raining down on us. Spiritual umbrellas usually hold up and shield us from smaller storms that simply come from being human.

Umbrellas can be short phrases representing sincerely held beliefs about life that allow people to feel protected until the actual crisis arrives. One of these umbrellas is "If you work hard, you will be rewarded." There are hundreds of these sayings that shape our worldviews though. What about this one: "If you love God and believe the Bible with all your heart, you can claim promises and make them yours"? Some of our principles are universal, some only work in America and are true most of the time, but that last statement, "claim promises and make them yours," is not biblical but cultural.

These false umbrellas that work for most storms quickly collapse when horrific accidents, mental illnesses, chronic disabilities, or health hurricanes hit our lives. God doesn't promise to shield you from all harm, regardless of how positive you are about life. We often prop up our Americanized version of Christianity with Bible verses that were never intended to serve that purpose. In a literal hurricane, anything not anchored down can become a projectile and create damage, and umbrellas are one such item. The same happens in people's hearts when Bible verses are misused. They become weapons to deny God's love for people walking through loss.

Thank God we were safe from cancer storms, or so we thought. We were a good family living wholly devoted to God's will. We thought we had God's favor, and we definitely thought scriptures promised protection. It's not that we believed we were better than anyone else, but we had taught our kids that God would provide protection against certain things, like dying from cancer in your twenties. The grief is still raw, and this storm ripped off the roof of our shallow assumptions about God, suffering, and faith. We had superficial and cultural features to a faith that left us clinging to a worldview that opposed the troubled life Jesus had warned about.

———————

Shortly after news of the cancer diagnosis spread around the church and my leadership circles, my office began to receive large and small boxes from all over the country. Supplements, unique and special waters, and expensive organic foods of all varieties came to my office monthly. Although well-intentioned, our family also began receiving other people's health umbrellas, which allowed them to keep a distance from our storm. The senders weren't close enough to our family to know we had been eating clean for two decades, and even though their words never said it, their love-motivated actions were inaccurately shaming the victim. *If you had done right, Whitney, or if you were in charge of your eating habits, you would not have been hit with cancer.* Despite their best intentions, it all implied that they were cancer-free because they had found the secret.

In her book *Suffering and the Heart of God,* Diane Langberg says, "The first thing I learned early on in my life was that suffering *is.* I learned that health is never certain, that maintaining it is often not under our control, and that disease, suffering, and pain can rise up out of nowhere and completely alter a life. I saw that health is not worthy of our worship, for it is a tentative, changeable and often fragile god."[24] It's human nature to construct protections around ourselves, and we hold to them until they don't work. Most of the time the only thing we have to hand to someone facing a horrible storm is a flimsy umbrella. There are some personal hurricanes for which an umbrella of any kind—religious, biological, philosophical, or any other kind—is no help at all.

Somewhere in life, someone you love will get hit by a storm that damages their life and threatens their faith. Every Floridian knows instinctively, an umbrella is not a sufficient line of defense against a hurricane. These storms will inevitably hit families whether they are attending church or not, making charitable donations or not, singing emotional love songs to Jesus or ancient hymns or not singing at all. Bonhoeffer said in *Letters and Papers from Prison,* "We must learn to regard people less in the light of what they do or omit to do, and more in the light of what they suffer."[25] Yet, identifying with someone in pain doesn't fit our conversion model, as we tend to pay more attention to their personal behavior rather than their sufferings. We try to offer fixes instead of offering comfort.

Some of the umbrellas handed to me in seminary did not work in our cancer hurricane. Christians can love God as sincerely as they know how, believe the Bible, adjust their lives to it and still not get a prayer answered. One might even feel genuinely convinced all Bible verses are God's promises for them and their family, only to be let down. I'm writing partially because of this challenging and uncomfortable reality. I raised my kids and other people's kids on these umbrellas.

Jesus told His followers that He had to go away so that the Comforter would come.[26] Think about it: the Miracle Worker says, "You don't need a miracle worker in this life; what you need is a comforter." But just how would this comfort be delivered? Not through Sunday sermons or rule following but through the personal closeness of His Spirit. The Holy Spirit didn't save them from suffering; rather the Comforter stayed with them in the suffering.

Jesus' resurrection did not shield His followers from earthly storms. They experienced suffering in God's name; they were imprisoned, beaten, stoned, flogged, and exiled. Though God was with them through it all, many were killed because of their faith. Jesus did not leave them with an umbrella; He didn't tell them they would be protected from all of life's storms if they had enough faith. No, He sent a comforter, His presence with them through everything to guide them into truth and to glorify Him in the midst of every storm.

Jesus told His followers, "Anyone who listens to my teaching and follows it is wise, like a person who builds a house on solid rock. Though the rain comes in torrents and the floodwaters rise and the winds beat against that house, it won't collapse because it is built on bedrock."[27] Wit went through her storm with a faith that did not collapse. Now the rest of the family lives daily in the collapsed hopes and expectations to hold her grandchildren and eat some of her low-glycemic recipes during the holidays. All of us now must see how we can withstand our personal storms of grief, pain, anger, confusion, and theological mystery as the floods and winds batter our own houses of faith.

Scripture tells us, "It is the glory of God to conceal a matter, to search out a matter is the glory of kings."[28] There are things you don't know, and this is a good phrase to say when you are seated beside someone on the mourning bench in a cemetery. Shallow answers, misappropriated Bible verses, or avoiding the reality that we will all die at some point are not helpful in the really bad storms of life. A theology of escapism or "Jesus suffered so I don't have to" mentality is just not true and will often leave you devastated. God always hears our prayers but doesn't always give us what we want. And when you see someone not get what they've prayed for, it's not God disciplining them; it just means God didn't give them what they asked for.

No matter their age, people love to get what they want. While willing a way might work in real estate and putt-putt golf, it doesn't work in the realm of spirituality. The stories and verses in the Bible are for you but not written *to* you. There are some stories and verses that won't apply to you whether you quote them, journal them, or say them out loud. One example would be to think of Psalm 91:

> *If you say, "The Lord is my refuge,"*
>   *and you make the Most High your dwelling,*
> *no harm will overtake you,*
>   *no disaster will come near your tent.*
> *For he will command his angels concerning you*
>   *to guard you in all your ways.*[29]
> *"Because he loves me," says the Lord, "I will rescue him;*
>   *I will protect him, for he acknowledges my name.*
> *He will call on me, and I will answer him;*
>   *I will be with him in trouble,*
>   *I will deliver him and honor him.*

With long life I will satisfy him
and show him my salvation."[30]

The words are poetic, inspired, and essential, but not a personal promise. Read it slowly and carefully, all of it, and you will realize the same thing. No prophet, pastor, or ordinary human can control God, regardless of how devoted they live. Wit once said, "The motive in which we approach the Bible will greatly affect our interpretation of it." This is very true of everyone individually and the American church. We can read the Bible through only the lens of prosperity, miracles, and certainty and find that when the storm comes, we are left with flimsy umbrellas that don't hold up under the weight of the suffering and grief that are inevitable in life.

———————

Hunkered down in a laundry closet for about eighteen hours, we got to witness the early stages of Whitney's default when things grew difficult. She always loved singing, making up songs, singing tunes that were new to us. During that hurricane, with the power out, this twelve-year-old began to sing a song her mom would sing with her when she was young and afraid of Florida thunderstorms. With her black and white shih tzu puppy on her lap she sang courageously, quiet at first and then louder:

Who's in the middle of a storm, God is
Who's in the middle of a storm, God is
Who's in the middle of a storm, God is
I'm not afraid 'cause God's in the middle of a storm!

We all sang with her for a while to drown out the awful noises you hear during a hurricane like Charley. It would turn out that Wit would use music to summon strength not only during unpredictable weather events but cancer storms too. As for the hurricane of Primary Progressive Refractory Hodgkin's Lymphoma, she was confident that God was going to heal her and share with others how God rescued her from the storm of cancer. But God's power did not show up with a miracle and neither her faith and hope, nor ours, was able to make that happen.

God was in the middle of the storm with her. Honestly, this is where some can't grasp the complexity and depth of our small family's suffering. Yes, we miss Whitney and grieve the unthinkable loss of our "baby girl." Yet at least for now, the even harder part is that the all-powerful God did nothing to stop the hurricane and have mercy on a young woman who just wanted to lead worship and have babies of her own. God allowed this hurricane to hit our home and dismantle the life we knew and the future life we expected to have with our daughter, and no humanly constructed umbrella could shield us from the relentless winds of sorrow.

Our family and yours are not the only people to be hit by these storms. Twentieth-century pastor and theologian Dietrich Bonhoeffer is said to have written just before he was executed by the Nazis, "We keep thinking that we ourselves will be spared when disaster strikes—until it is too late. . . . it explains our insensitivity toward the suffering of others; solidarity with suffering arises in proportion to our own increasing fear of imminent doom."[31] Suffering is inevitable, and the miracle doesn't always come, but in every storm we have a choice. We can choose faith in the mysterious God, or we can choose to let fear and grief separate us from Him. We can choose to sing and worship in uncertainty, like Wit did.

Wit's ability to continue singing in life's worst storms, in God's silence, in suffering, displays the depth of her faith and belief in God. She had wisdom to know God was with her in the storm, integrity to share her hope in God with others even during the scariest storms of her life, and tenacity to keep singing and inspiring others.

WISDOM MOMENT

On a blank page in your notebook or journal, name a storm that you are experiencing or one from your past that comes to mind. Jot down a few sentences about your expectations and any promises God has made to you.

INTEGRITY MOMENT

Name one umbrella you were handed in your past that you thought would help you during a storm but let you down. Record who or what has disappointed you the most in handling the big storms of life. What can you learn about God from that storm?

TENACITY MOMENT

Wit's story reminds us God is in the middle of your storm. He will never leave you or abandon you. Yes, it's possible He won't rescue you from the storm, but He will give you help to endure the storm and the energy to make a life afterward. Finish this sentence:

Dear God, I need some help with…

PART II

PRAYERS OF
THE GRIEVING

CHAPTER 4

BROKEN WINGS AND WEEPING ANGELS

You move me, O Lord, seeing you nailed to a cross and reviled; I am moved by the sight of your wounded body; I am moved by your sufferings and your death.[32]

—Lope de Vega

Wit's seventh birthday was approaching, and so was the end of her first-grade year. By Mother's Day, Darla was done with most of the planning for Wit's party. Just a year earlier, she had moved Wit and all the rest of us to gluten-free to eliminate whole grains and bad sugar from all our diets. Imagine a first-grader who never ate pizza, Pop-Tarts, Oreo cookies, or had birthday cake at her friends' parties. Yet, the transition to a gluten-free diet earlier that year had gone smoothly because of Wit's mom's care and imagination in the kitchen providing tasty alternatives. This former Marketing Director and watercolor artist learned to make food from scratch in the kitchen for the most important people in her life: her family. She had worked hard to make Wit feel like a normal kid, even making gluten-free cookies look like regular cookies for her class parties.

While Mom planned the party, Wit started planting gift ideas weeks ahead of the big day. This year she was asking for a bird. We were dog people. And even though we were not a cat family, we most certainly were not bird people. She had worked on her mom and me separately, trying to convince us to get her a bird for her birthday. Figuring out this food allergy had made the school year tough, and now Ms. Gluten-Free, straight A's, heading into the second grade all grown up, felt she deserved a bird. And a bird cage.

"Nice try. Wrong family. Not this year. We're too busy. We have a dog." I gave the same speech with some variation each time Wit asked. Her mom was also firm about the fact she could not get a bird. Each time she fruitlessly petitioned, she trudged away with her shoulders slumped.

Later we found out that Wit had gone behind our backs and appealed to a higher power for the bird. She asked for God to give her a bird for her birthday, even if her parents would not.

"Thank You, God," she said one fateful May morning. The four of us were playing in the backyard before the Orlando sun really heated up. The only shade was under the pacific cedar treehouse and slide.

"What is it, Wit?" I asked. She dropped to her little brown knees, pointing under the slide to a baby mourning dove. To this day, I have no idea how it got there. We had no trees inside the tall white privacy fence.

At first, I thought it was dead, so I put my hand on Wit's back to console her. She moved her face closer to the bird and said, "He blinked. He's alive!" The poor little guy was barely alive. I thought it would be better to let it die at a veterinarian's office than in front of our nature lover. I sent her after a shoebox so we could take it to the vet. The bird and box never met, as she cradled the bird in a towel the entire way. We learned from the receptionist that they won't treat wild birds. So, "head to the pet store down the street" was the professional medical advice.

The bird was between three and thirteen days old because there were no feathers, only fuzz. "Probably dropped by a hawk or predator of some kind," the pet store clerk said in a matter-of-fact tone, while loading a syringe with formula substitute. *Wow, that's a pretty dark and graphic thing to tell a seven-year-old*, I thought to myself. "A mother dove digests seeds before feeding them to her young, and since parrots are seed eaters, baby parrot food formula is the solution." Dog people just don't know these kinds of things.

The official diagnosis from the minimum-wage clerk at the pet store was a broken wing, needing eight weeks of care before we'd know if the bird would ever fly. As we walked back to the minivan with a syringe, special pre-feather tubing, parrot formula, a few other trinkets, and a bird with a broken wing, I realized God answered Wit's prayer—usurped our parental authority and gave her a bird. Wit willed that little bird back to life over the next few hours and days. She cared for him constantly and held him the whole time at her birthday party. She cradled that wounded animal night and day. She kept him safe in her hands and would not let anyone hold him, except for Mom. Wit would sing to this Zenaida macroura bird, that's the official name of the mourning dove, constantly.

Wit and I talked about her bird a few years before her death, when we were in Rome together with the family. It came up because we noticed the volume of wild birds seemed greater than in the States. At certain times of the year, we heard that people use umbrellas to shield themselves from getting dropped on by the birds, which is a common problem for some outdoor tourist attractions like the one that contains the sculpture of the famous *Angel of Grief*, or the *Weeping Angel*. The *Weeping Angel* is a famous sculpture carved by William Wetmore Story in 1894, at the grave of his wife, Emelyn, at the Protestant Cemetery in Rome.[33]

Story wrote about the sculpture, "It represents the angel of Grief, in utter abandonment, throwing herself with drooping wings and hidden face over a funeral altar. It represents what I feel."[34] The cemetery, founded in 1716, sits five miles south of the Vatican and just across the River Tiber. It's a cemetery full of poets and painters, sculptors and authors, and famous diplomats.

I believe heaven weeps over suffering; after all, Jesus wept at the news of a friend who had passed.[35] Suffering as a surviving family member means living with more questions than answers, more mystery than certainty, and trusting a voice you can't see. Faith is tested most when your heart is broken. The heart must decide to still trust God when the weeping won't stop, when it's dark with no light at all on the inside, and even when we have questions about God that the church can't answer.

Suffering is personal, nuanced, and complicated, and yet it's universal. Regardless of where you live, go to church, or what victories you have in life, suffering and grief will always be a part of your story. Wit and her lived experiences have taught me more about divine love, divine selflessness, and now divine grief than all my religious educational journey. Suffering has now come to us. Misery and suffering are a part of people's lives, and when Jesus came to Earth they filled His life too. I'm disappointed that I didn't hear more about Jesus' own misery and suffering in seminary or on Sundays.

Some church attendees hear far more on success, leadership, and creating personal achievement with positive attitudes than on the prevalence of suffering. I don't remember Jesus ever talking about success, positive attitudes, creating achievement, but suffering was a common theme throughout His life. The takeaway from most churches on Sundays, whether intentional or not, is that Christians are never supposed to lose. Christians are winners, right? Yet the real words of Jesus contradict that shallow mindset. Matthew 16:25 says, "For whoever wants to save their life will lose it, but whoever loses their life for me will find it." The greater narrative of God and His appearance on Earth as Jesus tells a very different story from the success we generally hear about. Christians are not winners but losers—at least in this life.

It is amazing to me that we've allowed such a progressive, contemporary application of Jesus' ministry to impact our view of God (theology) to the extent that we can't allow the message of suffering, difficulty, and pain to even enter our Sunday topics unless we promise deliverance and winning. There was a time when I'd much rather preach on the power of positive thinking, showing lots of grit, and climbing Mt. Everest with no oxygen than slowing down to make faith accessible to those in wheelchairs and with various other challenges, including the deep scars of grief and wounds from unanswered prayers.

With years of Sunday messages of God's goodness and faithfulness filed away, it can be extremely jarring when you experience suffering that completely alters the image of God you held. If you don't know the God who grieves with you—who suffered for you—then you are positioned to feel betrayed, alone, and knocked off course when suffering comes. When we walk with the God who grieves with us, we still walk through the valley of the shadow of death, but we are not alone: He is the light in the utter darkness; He is the presence with us on the mourning bench; He is the One who heals us, slowly, ever so slowly, through His loving presence.

Walking with God through grief is, as Wit sings in "This Path," both hard and good. The lyrics embody, almost like a foretelling, what was ahead for Whitney. The song is slow and melodic and feels troubling when she sings, "the shadows overtake," but then leads into this final firm declaration of "I'll walk with you." Wit's life was God's alone. Read the words and say them softly as you do so your ears can hear them too.

> *This path I'm walking on is hard and good, You stay right*
> *where you should, next to me. The morning breaks again,*

*and the birds sing their song, I join my voice with theirs,
how great, how good, we sing. I believe in your promises,
I believe you never leave. I believe in your promises, I
believe, Oh I believe.*

*The mountain goes high, and I can't see the top. I try to
enjoy the climb but it's just so rough. The valley goes deep,
and the shadows overtake. Still I trust in you, in the words
you speak. I believe in your promises, I believe you never
leave. I believe in your promises, I believe, Oh I believe.
I want to waste my life on you! To serve you! To love you!
When it's all said and done, I want to hear, Well Done! I
want to waste my life on you! To serve you! To love you!
When it's all said and done, I want to hear, Well Done!
Oh, oh, oh – ahhhh! I'll walk with you, I'll walk with you,
Oh…I'll walk with you, I'll walk with you, Oh…I want
to waste my life on you! To serve you! To love you! When
it's all said and done, I want to hear, Well Done! I want
to waste my life on you! To serve you! To love you! When
it's all said and done, I want to hear, Well Done!
This path I'm walking on is hard and good.*

That sweet melodic voice allows for the dark mystic rhythms of the
Spirit to enter the valley of the shadow of death, to be a pilgrim as it were
on a difficult journey. The veiled reference to the valley of the shadow
of death lurks eerily in the background, but she expresses resolutely in
the bridge that she will still walk with God. She's saying to God that no
matter how hard the path gets, it's a good path because it's the one He
chose. She confidently expresses that God stays right where He should,
next to her.

Those lyrics alone are enough to move the human heart toward a tighter connection between the path and God and the good He will do in the end. But Wit breaks out the most controversial, irreligious phrase, in a direct reference to the woman who poured very expensive perfume on Jesus, resulting in Judas shaming her in front of everyone. She declared "I want to waste my life on you," meaning to give Jesus everything you have, to anoint Him with your life, and to stand out for God no matter what others say! No fame or awards here, only a desire to walk with and worship the Creator.

Judas, as the narrative shows, was very much opposed to this waste of money but also its misuse.[36] They were in a small room and the aroma would have overpowered the atmosphere and probably drove everyone, save a few, outside. Wit's life, for as far back as I can remember, carried an aroma of compassion toward others, and her love of God, which revealed the source of her life.

Flowers must die for their aromas to exist beyond their life span. You lose the visual beauty of the flower for the invisible aroma to fill the room. I can't think of a significant person mentioned in the sacred Scriptures who did not experience difficulties, tragedy, or loss, and the Bible reveals what came out of them at the time. Scripture says that, like plants, we were made from the dirt and to the dirt we shall return.[37] When great pressure and pain are allowed into our lives, they press on us, and an essence or flavor emits from our lives whether we like it or not. We lost the visible presence of one of God's songbirds, or in this case peony flowers (Wit's favorite), as it was crushed under the weight of great suffering, and all we have left is the aroma of her life, worship, and faith. On this side of eternity, it all seems like a waste—the very thing she wrote in the song.

———————

There is a huge difference between belief in a kind and loving God who will never let you down and faith in a God who has suffered like you suffer. God's love for us is the solid ground, the foundation of all things; He is the One who gives us sure footing on the path that is hard and good. His is a perplexing love that does not keep the suffering and sorrow away but is extravagant in the strength it offers to us. The path of grief is not linear, and sometimes you'll find yourself right back where you started. But God uses all things—the sorrow, the wailing, the lament, the questioning—to bring you into a deeper knowledge of Him and healing of your mind and spirit.

Pain, internal suffering, is the door that leads down the long, winding staircase into the deeper parts of human existence. In this space, we can see God's overwhelming grace extended to His creation. It's the only door leading to resurrection. The good news is that the greater the depth of your sorrow, the closer and more intimate opportunity you have to become one with Christ. You die to the things of this world that are only temporary as you share in His sufferings. A careful reading of Jesus' invitation to His followers reveals a long, slow descent down the staircase into a suffering kind of life. And yet, it's not a morbid invitation but one to dig deep in the ground of God where new life blossoms again. Jesus said, "Very truly I tell you, unless a kernel of wheat falls to the ground and dies, it remains only a single seed. But if it dies, it produces many seeds."[38]

One day I vividly remember talking with Wit about spiral staircases in a magnificent, palatial home. As you spiral around down into the cellar from the top floor, you walk in a circle, seeing all the same things from a different perspective. Life in God is a descent into the foundation of existence, which is love for God and others. Suffering and pain may make it feel as if you are walking in circles, but you are actually descending into the servanthood of Christ. We learn to understand Him better as we see Him from different perspectives, experience Him in different ways. This is one reason Jesus said "the last will be first."[39] The further you go down the staircases, the more the sunlight disappears; things are colder and darker, but God is at work in you even in the place where you can't make sense of things with your mind.

We all rejoice with those who declare they received a miracle. However, I've found some, but not all, of those testimonies are somewhat exaggerated—and they usually do collateral damage to families who stood in faith, blocked all negativity and doubt, and lived fully devoted only to not get a miracle. Were they somehow not worthy of a miracle? In these cases of God's inactivity, usually two options emerge: the family members either blame God or blame themselves. However, I believe a third option is more biblical: people should expect suffering and trouble in this life as the norm. Expect that God will never leave you alone in it and that He will comfort you by His Spirit. This option allows no blaming, just enduring on the narrow trail through the steep mountain of grief.

You can take my hand now as I walk you down the staircase into a darker place that we humans are most fearful of—it's the dying place. It will put your faith at risk and expose the false narratives you've carried that tell you you're protected from bad things in this life. But this truth isn't cause to worry, as our Guide is leading us down into this place where newness and greatness from heaven's view exists. After some time, we come to see only Him and that He alone is our light—and that is enough.

History shows us that God did not stand far off and reach out to us but came and walked around inside the suffering human experience and led the way down. He endured the anguish of the garden and the cross. New creation is waiting to be born in all of us and reunite us all one day into an even larger family if we are willing to die to what we want and to pray, "not my will, but yours be done."[40]

"His name shall be Chucky!" Wit had grown so close to this little dove that she had to name it. This naming represented a change in their relationship. I prayed over Wit every night as I had from her birth—and of course for the bird now too—that God would put a song in Wit's heart and keep the song going for little Chucky. She had become a momma to this wild bird, caring for it night and day. Chucky lived in the box with no lid, under her lamp, right beside her for a few months.

Soon after the naming, she told us excitedly that his wing seemed fine and healthy and came up with the idea to set him free all on her own. True to her word, she released Chucky in the backyard. He would fly to the fence and sit for long periods of time and fly around the yard. Sometimes he would land on Wit's shoulder and other times her head. She would giggle with joy, and we watched in amazement as we realized something otherworldly was taking place right in our backyard. Chucky would not leave. My wife confirms that it took more than three weeks to get him to fly away for good. Wit would sit on the patio near the climbing equipment for hours, watching Chucky, and then she would take him back upstairs to her room for the night and try releasing him again the next day.

God stays right with you during your trouble and trauma. Our world is fraught with harshness, trouble, and cruelty, and none of us want to fly out into the real world, just like Chucky didn't want to leave Wit. Although the world is wild, there is a God who is close and faithful but just out of view. He is the God who provides wholeness to us, which is a divine healing of the heart, soul, and mind. We should always pray and expect for people to get a miracle, but I'll be right there for them if they don't get one—encouraging them to not equate God's presence with the lack of a supernatural rescue moment.

God was there with Wit during every chemotherapy appointment and, even more important, during those difficult phone calls after the scans. God had named Whitney, put a song in her heart, and cradled her tenderly in His loving hands, just like she did with Chucky. She knew the God who overruled parents and gave her a dove. He is also the God who did not stop the suffering or the cancer. He is still the God this family serves. He holds us in the mornings when we wake up in tears. He is the suffering God who not only knew Wit's pain and sorrow firsthand but knows ours too. He chose to give us the miracle of His presence rather than a miracle over cancer, and we will have to be okay with that. Agreeing with that decision and liking the outcome is another thing altogether, but for me, this is where faith comes into play.

There will come a moment when you really have to decide whether or not you will have real faith. Do you believe God loves you? Don't allow the pain, suffering, and sorrow in this world to rob you of that belief. His love is close in the pain, and God is with us in our here and now. "So then, since we have a great high priest who has entered heaven, Jesus the Son of God, let us hold firmly to what we believe. . . . so let us come boldly to the throne of our gracious God. There we will receive His mercy, and we will find grace to help us when we need it most."[41]

Your life will have more weeping angels in it than people will tell you. Your life will be more about endurance than living life physically pain free. When the suffering feels like too much, and you feel like God has forsaken you, know that He is right there with you, holding you and grieving with you. Wit walked this path with the wisdom to know God was always with her, the integrity not to veer off path when every day was an uphill battle, and the tenacity to waste her life continually and gloriously on the loving God who was present with her through it all.

WISDOM MOMENT

The wisdom we seek today is to exchange childish, Disney-like theology for a deeper biblical wisdom. When Wit named her bird, it represented a change in their relationship. Have you ever called God by name? The word "God" functions more like a title, but Jesus was fully God. Write out the name "Jesus" on a page of your journal. If any images or stories come to mind, jot them down. If not, spend some time staring at that name as you sip on a warm drink, and ask for wisdom today.

INTEGRITY MOMENT

When you read the story of Wit and her bird, which character were you most like in the story? Wit, Chucky, the parents, the pet store clerk, or the veterinarian's office?

TENACITY MOMENT

Tenacity will come easier once you know your identity. Answer the following questions yes or no and record any thoughts that come to mind. God is a trustworthy Father. God is good-natured. God knows your name.

CHAPTER 5
THE WAILING WALL

For myself, I declare I don't know anything about it. But the sight of the stars always makes me dream.[42]

—Vincent van Gogh

On a summer vacation in the mountains, Wit and I made a pact one night that I'd go with her to feed breakfast to the ducks. Morning light barely lit the kitchen as we sat at the table and carefully broke the bread into fragments. It filled three paper plates to their maximum capacity. Through the screen door and down the squeaky wooden steps, the moon shadows were giving way to first light.

"Here's the plan, Dad. Don't feed any ducks until I tell you." She talked fast about a small duck she was concerned was not getting enough food because of all the competition. "I am worried about him," she said. "You feed all of the other ducks, and keep them close to you." As we walked toward the water's edge, more than a dozen ducks started swimming across the cove toward us. I noticed the one duck far behind the others and followed her instructions.

The mounds of bread pieces on the paper plate clearly caused a lot of excitement out in the water. And as the invasion began, some of the ducks started climbing out of the water, nipping at my shoes. Wit—in her kind but firm voice—kept saying to wait. I did. She was twenty feet away when finally the little duck arrived, and she said, "Now." I began dropping the bread pieces as planned. Wit was really taking her time dropping one piece of bread at a time into the water, all of it just out of sight of the ducks near me. Once I had dispensed my bread, I approached Wit and her little friend. What I saw was a one-legged duck. He was missing a flipper. He had learned to compensate and not swim in circles and seemed especially grateful to Wit.

What I experienced in that moment sticks with me to this day. At the time, we were planting a church in Orlando, and I was driving forty-three miles every day to teach at a university to support us. I would leave the house before the kids were up and make the commute for my early classes. Planting near Disney and SeaWorld was not easy and made purchasing real estate and renting the local middle school for church every week nearly financially impossible.

That morning on the dock with Wit, my thoughts were simple: Since a five-year-old can notice a one-legged duck, prepare food in the dark, set a specific time to deliver provision, recruit a helper, and pay special attention to the one needy duck—we would have what we needed to plant this church. The God-nature I saw in Wit came from the same God who would provide for the church and our family during the planting season. Wit took pleasure in making sure the animals did not just have food but got the attention they deserved. And now, in our present suffering without Wit, I pray that God would help us not to swim in circles but to finish our lives with purpose.

Psalm 116:15 says, "Precious in the sight of the Lord is the death of his faithful servants." And pastors repeat it sincerely, thinking that it will offer comfort. Maybe it does when your ninety-nine-year-old great-grandmother dies but not when you lose a child. Wit's passing was tough, and it ended poorly in the physical realm, her body racked with pain. We all just had the sense that this was not right. We could do nothing to save her, and God chose not to. This was too harsh of an ending for someone like Wit, who was so kind to people and all of God's creation. She left us at twenty-seven, and all she had ever wanted was to have babies and lead worship. Nothing about her death seemed precious.

Wit was fun and funny, artsy and poetic, and full of love for everyone and everything God created. She was a truth-teller, which demands authenticity from me in sharing her story. Her premature death feels like an injustice. It's like our prayers just hit the wall. It's a wall that seemed to block the prayers for a miracle from reaching God's heart. It's a wall that the whole family, including Wit herself, dealt with the whole time, and the wall I still sense at times as I walk down this path of grief.

––––––––––––

One of the most familiar landmarks in the land of Israel is known as the Wailing Wall. Of all the things God did for the Jewish people over the centuries, all the miracles and sea crossings and food drops from the sky, their most well-known landmark is a wall where people cry—that can't be good.

The Wailing Wall or the Western Wall is a remnant of the temple, which since its conception has represented the presence of God to the Jewish people. One time a year, they believed God would come down and visit with them via the temple; they believed it was where heaven and Earth communed.

The first temple was constructed during King Solomon's reign and was believed to be the place where God would always live. One thousand years later, Jesus would walk those sacred spaces. Jesus had come to be the Jewish people's King but told them the throne would be in their hearts and not an earthly temple. Jesus knew the Jewish people didn't like being under Roman oppression and wanted to make their nation great again like in Solomon's day. Jesus knew that the physical landmark of the temple that the people put their faith in was nothing compared to the power of His presence in their lives and the promise of His spirit. Jesus prophesied before His death that the temple would be destroyed and He would rebuild it in three days.[43] He was of course referring to His body and the resurrection that would change the world forever.

Eventually, the physical temple was also destroyed by the Romans, and only one wall remained. The Western Wall of the place where humanity and God connected was all that was left standing. And over time, it gained a reputation of being a place where God's followers would come to pray and wail, the physical wall representing a spiritual blockage felt in many people's hearts. The Jews had to continually live with the reminder that their holy temple was down to a few stones stacked up together. The people who visit the Wailing Wall today in Jerusalem roll up little paper sheets with prayers written on them and wedge them into the cracks of what used to be.

Just saying the word "wailing" out loud is a little disturbing. It's not a word we use often and nearly everyone knows that it means someone is making sounds from deep in their belly. I can imagine someone describing wailing to someone wholly unfamiliar with the concept by saying it is a prolonged mournful sound coming from an invisible place of suffering. Wails don't just happen at walls but every place in the world where war, hunger, separation, or disease has entered the human experience. I also know that I had never heard wailing until I listened to my wife sob the morning Wit left us. I can't un-hear it; it was haunting and unnerving but authentically how she felt—how we all felt—about Wit's death.

We prayed four years for God to heal, and to be brutally honest, sometimes it felt like we were praying to a wall. We never got an answer while we prayed, and her suffering was not minimized or relieved as far as we could tell. The Hodgkin's Lymphoma seemed in charge and not God. Her death removed the understanding of a nice and loving God that would never allow this family unit to be ripped apart. Our prayers look pretty empty now because they didn't work or bring any change (that we are aware of) during those four years. But we are finding an unusual inner strength we have because of all those prayers; the power of God's presence produced a humility to trust Him. I think now it was His presence that, even though we didn't get our miracle, causes us to respond like the faithful Jewish people who still go pray at the wall.

We were at a restaurant a few weeks after Wit died, and the server, trying to make light conversation, asked us, "How many children do you have?" This innocent question of someone making small talk turned on the faucet of tears and pierced our hearts. At the time we had never contemplated how we would have to learn to answer that question. Now, months later, we realize that we still have two children. One is here, and one now lives outside our daily awareness, but we still have two kids. So, we always respond to questions like that with the quick answer of, "Two!" But the question will always be a painful reminder of what we lost. Nearly every day, something like that happens. It reminds us that there's now a wailing wall right in the middle of our lives, and we have to walk past it every day. Some days we sit down at the wall and grieve and other days we choose to pass it by, but it's always visible.

I am coming to see that most people will experience some event or calamity that will bring them to the metaphorical wailing wall in their lives, often when they least expect it. The wall represents lostness, what used to be, the way things were, and a comfortable way of life. When you experience a profound loss, you are not just grieving what you lost but losing what never will be. You are continually grieving a future that never became reality.

It is possible to pray and pray and pray and not see any results. It's even biblical. I know that's not what you usually hear on Sundays. Prayer, some have said, moves the hand of God. While that might be true for some people who pray, it wasn't for us. Prayer with food, prayer without

>

food, carpet-sucking prayer, and all-night prayer did not change the out-come science had predicted all four years. Our experience aligns more with those standing at the wall of presence, disappointed that it's all they have left. And yet, God's presence, just like Jesus promised, powerfully soothes our hurting hearts every day. Most days we can feel a Presence with us, helping us endure another day.

Although we are just into the second year of coping with Wit being gone, we have found strength in the truth-telling messages from Rick and Kay Warren, pastors who lost their twenty-seven-year-old son Matthew to mental illness. Their integrity, humility, and generosity have always been something Darla and I have admired from a distance. We don't know them personally, but their vulnerability publicly has been priceless for our wounded hearts. They also prayed for years for a mira-cle and stood on certain Bible verses with great faith and fervent prayer. The thing we will always appreciate about them is their openness in pro-cessing their pain and using it to help people like us and so many others.

Rick and Kay talk often about the shock of losing their son and how shock is often the first stage of loss.[44] Recently, my daughter-in-law, Heather, said, "We never realized how much faith we had for Whitney's healing until we realized that we had never contemplated her death." To this day, much of our suffering is rooted in the fact that we spent four years praying that God would heal Wit, never expecting that He would not. The shock of her death is still a stage that we pass through on some days, and as I look around, I see many other parents and family members wailing over who they've lost. In her book *The Unspeakable Loss*, Nisha Zenoff speaks of the grief of losing a child. My experiences in many ways align with her descriptions.

> *The grief process is neither uniform nor linear. After some better days, we may find ourselves circling back to a place of indescribable pain. Another day, our dark mood lifts.*

We circle forward and back in this dance of grief, with
the only constant being change itself. I encourage you to
respect your individual grief/healing process, to trust that
you are healing as you are meant to.[45]

After two years without Wit, we keep finding ourselves back at the wailing wall, every day more deeply understanding that the path of grief is not linear but almost spiral in nature—taking us back to the same place often. We find ourselves on our knees, staring, praying, wailing at the immovable. What took some time for me to figure out is that grieving isn't a race or destination; you can't just walk faster or work harder and finish the grieving process. As I keep finding myself back at the wailing wall, I have come to realize I have a wall in my life, and I can worship at it or I can curse at it but either way, it's not moving.

He was handsome, this twenty-five-year-old, born a van Gogh. All he ever wanted in life was to become a preacher like his father, but you rarely hear that about Vincent. Vincent's first pastoral assignment was also his last. He was assigned to a poor mining village called Borinage. Located about three hundred miles north of Paris in a very poor area of the country of Belgium, he began to fulfill his call to preach the Bible and stayed for two years. He grew a deep love for the people there, the hungry and suffering miners and peasants. He tried hard to rescue people from poverty by giving away nearly all his earthly possessions to help these destitute souls suffering in the late 1800s.

Church politics pushed Vincent from priest to painter in a short two years.[46] Van Gogh was distraught over his rejection from the church and writes about his broken heart to his brother Theo. He left the church like so many others, embittered and broke. He told his brother Theo about the church, "I wish they'd simply accept me as I am."[47] He was tormented from this time forward and, sadly, is known by his long bouts with mental anguish. The suffering internally, and I believe spiritually too, was so pronounced that he had numerous breakdowns and in one episode cut off much of his ear. Though his experience with the church caused great suffering, his faith in God remained. In one letter to his brother, he shared Victor Hugo's quote, "Religions pass, but God remains."[48]

My love for art came through my wife, Darla, an art student, teacher, and watercolor artist herself. Her depth of art history knowledge helped me connect my understanding of the art world with my knowledge of the church, and to ultimately discover Vincent, this Dutch post-impressionistic painter who hardly sold a work while alive. He painted the peasants and the poor, reflecting his God-given compassion for their suffering. He created about 2,100 pieces of art and gave his brilliance to the world. He was a sometimes-disturbed person whose religion let him down. He expected more from the church and its leaders and never found the peace that he searched for in his work. This brokenhearted pastor and preacher painted what most consider his most popular piece in 1889 called The Starry Night. Van Gogh said of this piece, "For my part I know nothing with any certainty, but the sight of the stars makes me dream."[49]

––––––––––––

The high school in North Carolina Wit attended was not congruent with her love of the underdog and her overall compassionate view of life. It was a pretty dog eat dog world. She was always an A student, except in math, but it was all the stuff taking place before, between, and after the classes that caused her stress. She texted me these words on her first phone in 2008, just after she had finished some quiet time with God alone after getting home from school. I pasted the words into my journal. Here's the full unedited text I received:

There are moments in life that are disappointing. There are moments that make you sick and moments that make you smile. My life consists of moments that are both good and bad. Today I feel lonely and discouraged. Yesterday I felt connected and positive. I think how I perceive those moments are influenced by my emotions. So, what does that mean? It means to live aware of my emotions and how frequently they will change. It means that I should enjoy the good moments and push through the bad moments. It means that when I think it will never get better, hold on because it will. And when I think it can't get worse that it will, just hold on. But through any kind of moment there has to be a solid foundation I stand on, so that I don't let my emotions control or define who I am. What is there in this life that is solid and I can trust? Nothing. Which means I have to trust in something further than this world; which means believing in something greater than myself. That something greater is God. That something greater gives hope, grace, love, and valuable lessons that I don't want to learn. So, today I have to smile when I think about the blessings that God has surrounded me with and forget about the negative. The negative emotions are constantly changing, just as the positive are.

Even as a fifteen-year-old, Wit was learning to endure the emotional pain of this life. A simple overview of the Bible shows that the very people God wanted to use to reveal Himself to the world suffered and experienced wailing times too. God's people suffered throughout history; they always have and always will. Cancer and all other types of suffering too alter your life forever. If you have suffered a loss, you don't ever get over it; you get through it one day at a time. Some days you work hard to breathe and cope and eventually integrate the pain into your life as it is now.

Jesus' disciples, Van Gogh, and Wit all learned not to put their trust in institutions, buildings, and other man-made things. If you want to lean on something with the full weight of your suffering, it needs to be sturdier than a crumbling wall. Wit trusted in God's presence in her life, from the time she was five years old, caring for ducks, to fifteen years old, navigating the rough waters of high school, to twenty-seven years old, fighting for every breath. She leaned fully into God, trusting in Him and His plan.

My faith has so far survived the loss of my beautiful daughter—I've learned to lean on God as I watched Wit do. Watching cancer ravage someone you love pushes your faith to the breaking point. Knowing an all-powerful God is standing by, refusing to help in a way you could notice, is hard to deal with on so many levels. Yet when I survey Jesus' life—One who was born into oppression and knew suffering like He did—I understand that He knows what Wit experienced. At the core of a mature faith, followers hold onto the hope that Jesus' painful and excruciating death mattered and made a way for all of us to be reunited one day with our loved ones. That is a hope the heart holds onto despite the brain telling you that it's just too impossible.

We believe in God Almighty, like the Apostles Creed states emphatically, but I've never heard anyone declare that they believe in God All-Suffering! The creeds and conventions were, for the most part, called and paid for by emperors who wanted the church's influence added to their own power. As they sought the association of the church, they wanted their own power reflected in the institutions they aligned themselves with. In other words, there was a desire to emphasize the power and kingship of God. Highlighting the all-suffering God would not have fit the overall desired outcome at that time. To call God All-Suffering, rather than or even alongside Almighty, would have implied weakness and, in the mindset of so many, sin.

Suffering and sin are not the same thing. The pattern of crucifixion present in people's lives often reflects the presence of faith, not the presence of sin. The cross was never a one-off event but rather Jesus stepping into the human condition and exposing what the enemy of our souls was up to—trying to convince us there was no hope. Jesus immediately provided for us a life that mirrors His—not free from suffering, but also not ending with suffering. We are given lives full of resurrection power now, not so that we don't suffer, but rather so that we understand how our suffering exposes our faith and reveals that God is making all things new. This is the power of God at work in us, now and forever.

When our lives are hit by suffering and God doesn't use His power to rescue us, our simple thinking leaves us to blame God, the devil, or ourselves. All blaming, even blaming the devil, still leaves us at a spiritual dead end. There is no heart transformation in that place, as pessimism mimics authenticity. It's so easy to default to jaded anger, endlessly searching for someone to blame. Our bad thinking about God gives us only one way to interpret what's happening when we suffer. The sad reality is that most, if not all, reading this book will at some point find themselves at a wailing wall. During that season, it will feel like your prayers aren't working and that nothing is changing. You might feel horrible on the inside or just be trying to navigate the numbness trauma has caused. At some point in your life, you may even hit a patch of trouble that feels like it might destroy you or your faith.

A normal American Christian, before Covid-19, would not have expected to live life pressing their face against the wailing wall of suffering, but some are seeing that even money can't stop a pandemic. My growing concern for sincere American Christians is that their Sunday learnings over the last decade have left them woefully unprepared to keep their faith while wailing at the wall. During the writing of this chapter, a frantic father called me with news that their son was climbing a mountain near us and the two safety clips attached to the rock had broken away. He plunged to the rocks below. At that moment, the young man was fighting for his life in the emergency room. People we know are being laid off from work, and another person's spouse lost their mobility and requires full-time home care. A young woman, not much older than Wit, miscarried again. Covid-19 has claimed the lives of five people close to us and a family member is on a ventilator and not doing well. Why won't God help stop the suffering that has come to us and all the other people experiencing similar things? We don't expect pain, suffering, and trouble for the most part—or we hope God will rescue us. When He doesn't, we find ourselves at the wailing wall, surrounded by those who are suffering and traveling their own paths of grief.

During times of grief, we often feel like a one-legged duck, swimming in circles and desperate for nourishment. This cyclical nature of grief leads us time and time again to the wailing wall, where our faith is tested and strengthened. God, like Wit with that duck, is watching over you. And His presence, the Comforter, is not in a physical place like a temple but dwells within you. The wailing walls of life show you that you are not in control, and you need comfort only God can deliver. Vincent van Gogh's sad story in my view also reveals that truth. The walls of suffering in our lives reveal just how overwhelming life can be and how much we need God's grace to get through each day. The process we are learning from Wit's story is to always ask for God's wisdom on your path of grief, to be full of integrity as you dialogue with God and others about the walls of sorrow in your life. We also learned from Wit to find the tenacity to continue coming to the wall and saying your prayers, knowing His presence will come and abide.

WISDOM MOMENT

Select one of the following ideas mentioned in this chapter and take several minutes to jot down tips in your journal on getting through your suffering today.

- Wailing Wall
- Baby duck
- Wit's text
- Van Gogh's quote under the chapter heading
- "Pray and pray with no results"
- "Pessimism mimics authenticity"

INTEGRITY MOMENT

How difficult is it for you to tell the truth about the doubts and uncertainty you are experiencing? Why do you think it's so challenging? Write out the thing you would most like to know from God but don't—and may never—have the answer to.

TENACITY MOMENT

Jot down at least one sincere prayer that was not answered or to which you didn't get the answer you wanted. Make a list and sit with it for a minute. Make yourself comfortable, maybe even grab a cup of your favorite hot beverage. Go slow and feel the emotions that pop up in your body as you contemplate those unanswered prayers. Perhaps anger, hurt, disappointment or something else has impacted the way you pray now. Reflect on and journal about those things.

CHAPTER 6

THE PRESENCE OF ABSENCE

We cannot live the afternoon of life according to the program of life's morning, for what was great in the morning will be little at evening and what in the morning was true, at evening will have become a lie.[50]

—Carl Jung

Wit lay on her tummy on the grass, legs peddling an invisible bike slowly behind her. Her little chin rested in her hands, singing to a butterfly as if it could hear. Appreciating the profound beauty of God's creations was easy. Her beautiful milky skin browning slowly as it did each spring. She loved the fall and winter seasons partly because the native Floridian wanted to see snow at some point during her year. She also loved them because she could wear layers and quirky hats. Her hair was thick, dark brown, and perfectly her, but the hats let her express another side to her complex self. Playfully mischievous, never negative, and always starting each day from a happy place are all things her close friends could confirm. The butterfly in its own glorious transformation had prophetically predicted—without my catching it at the time—Wit's own transformation too.

"The scan is finally clear!" she told us just three months after receiving the new experimental immunotherapy, and seventeen months before she passed. Our internal celebrations were hopeful but muted. We talked about it and decided to embrace it publicly so that we didn't insult God if this was the path to healing for us. We fully believed and declared her healing and celebrated, privately fighting off the gnawing feeling in our guts that it wasn't over. Wit even booked an Airbnb that very next week, planning what would end up being our final family trip together; this time she picked Vancouver Island. The week before we boarded our flights to go, she found out the cancer had returned, and we received an email that our Airbnb had caught fire and burned to the ground. Wit, resilient as always, got online and booked another place for what would end up being our last trip together.

She's gone. I've lost Earth time with her now. There are no butterflies on the island of sorrow. On the island, this dark night, God stays silent and passive in the background. Why allow this wounding of me, of us? I wrote in my journal one morning after looking back at photos of Brayden playing with his little sister, "I am a devastated dad on the carpet in my study who now knows nothing about answers to prayer. The sun not warm and the moon all dark. Deprived of God bearing light in the place where dads and moms lose a child. Religion is no help, only a bother here in the land where only truth can be told. It's the place where factual hunger and thirst for God are born." What we have now is the presence of her absence.

We had imagined God would not allow evil to hit our family. But that was not only not a promise from Him, but it also elevated our sorrow early on in the days of our grief. Sorrow can partially block our understanding of God and His love. Sorrow is not just a mental experience but an emotional one too; the sorrow made crueler by the insensitivity of other believers who have God all organized up and served out of to-go boxes for normal consumption. You see, many will say, "Whitney is healed now." No offense, but well, duh! I know she's okay now, and she's not dead but alive. But she is not here and was not healed. She died. Shallow vocabulary gymnastics won't work for a broken heart. I am sorry if that sounds bitter, but I feel the need to be a voice for all those who've experienced a great loss. I'm trying to expose shallow, television religion that doesn't work down here on the ground when dust returns to dust.

One incredible blessing of the suffering we walk through is the other side of the experiences of Bible characters and the narratives recorded about their lives. For example, very little went "right" for King David in his private life. He was completely unloved by his siblings, rejected by his father, resented by his children, and his first wife despised his love for God. I could go on and on, but now we see things in the Scriptures that never stood out to us before. The key thing we saw of David really was his relentless pursuit to love God with all his heart. He learned to tell God what he was going through and many psalms come from his personal pain expressed through poetry and song, just like my Wit's.

Since it was permissible for David to tell God the truth, regardless of how difficult, we should give each other permission to say without shame that we asked God for a miracle and He did not give us one. It's okay to say we prayed for healing but it did not manifest in this life. We need to take the mask off the Bible stories and let them speak for themselves; we need to read the stories of the oppressed and the suffering and not minimize their struggles or mitigate their pain through "happily ever afters."

We've created a magic bedtime story book, glossing over the gory parts and misappropriating stories to fit our current lifestyles. When people think and talk about King David, it is often through the lens of a brave man and warrior after God's own heart, a leader who made some missteps but always found redemption. No one ever talks about a God who chose a young boy, anointed him king, and then sent him into a bloody, violent encounter. Think about how bad things were in those days that you would sacrifice a young boy's innocence and steal away the rest of his childhood as his blood-spattered face finished hacking off Goliath's head with the giant's oversized sword. Not exactly the bedtime story you want to share with your kids, but it is the reality of the human condition.

He had victories but little joy, and the joy he did have in God's presence was generally sabotaged. Out of David's pain came intimate lyrics of songs this lonely man would sing into the sky, to the God he could not see. The psalms David wrote are revealing and meaningful, but most of them were written during and after great personal suffering. In that same way, our family asking God for a miracle and feeling overwhelmed by sorrow is like bringing down a giant of our own. We are battered by the realities of losing our daughter to cancer. We are still wiping off the blood spatters on our faces, only we didn't get to kill the giant—he killed the life we had come to know. But like David, we are changed by the encounter and have little inherent joy. Like David losing his innocence in taking Goliath's life, a Sunday morning religion that is tidy and reserved for one day a week or just Christmas or Easter has been stripped from our reality.

Grief slows the sense-making activity in the brain, and the soul catches weariness like a cold that lingers. The once-seeing heart must now wait in the dark. The sorrowful heart now sees the empty space where a devoted mom would rub the lymph nodes on her daughter's head and neck for two and three hours at a time. A mother's heart remembers, but her hands do too, experts now say. Which means Darla is literally covered in memories of loss and grief, on the inside and out, and from head to toe. Your sorrow, the pain you bear in your heart, is not just in the center of your emotions but stored within the body, all organized by the brain.[51]

The Theory of Chronic Sorrow appears first in the *Journal of Nursing Scholarship*. The findings indicate that pervasive sadness is common when feelings are associated with a significant loss and should be labeled as chronic sorrow. Chronic sorrow is activated by the presence of absence. The blend of one's experiences, trigger events, and ability to manage this pain elicit chronic sorrow. The importance of this is to know that chronic sorrow is a normal response to loss. In other words, part of being human is learning how to cope with the ongoing absence of your loved one.

In a *Journal of Nursing Scholarship* report, researchers found that 86 percent of caregivers to those with chronic illnesses and bereaved family members demonstrated characteristics of having chronic sorrow.

> *In bereavement situations, the disparity that triggers chronic sorrow is not the presence of a person with a chronic condition. Rather, it is the disparity from the ideal created by the absence of a person who was central in the life of the bereaved. Stated another way, for bereaved individuals, it is the presence of the absence that triggers chronic sorrow. The chronic sorrow experience for bereaved people is most frequently triggered by confrontation with disparity associated with memories of a past reality, often associated with anniversary events, and with recognized variances from social norms.*[52]

People outside the grief circle more easily understand the despondency we feel around holidays and birthdays. However, other important days that are ordinary to everyone else can create imaginary anniversaries in the mind of the person with chronic sorrow. The triggering comes from the absence of a person, not necessarily a specific memory or event of the past.

Around other people—especially those who have never suffered a great loss—I sometimes get the feeling that they are thinking, Why are you not over this by now? I understand their point of view because I used to see the world through those glasses. Yet, persistent periods of recurring sadness are a normal response to a great absence in your life. Once I asked a large audience how many can remember vividly the death of a special pet they had growing up and still think of the animal quite often, and hundreds of hands raised. If a pet can mean that much to a human, so much that they can still feel the absence or loss years later, how much more does a spouse or grieving person deserve our patience and understanding?

———————

Several years ago, a close friend invited me to attend some leadership meetings in Switzerland. When I shared with him the news of Wit's diagnosis, he graciously invited her to sing at the retreat. Words can't describe how much it meant to Wit to lead those few dozen global leaders in worship a few hundred yards up from Lake Geneva on the border between France and Switzerland. Some present were facing great suffering in their own lives and families. The same emotion I had seeing Wit sing to a butterfly when she was young came upon everyone in the room—this moment of realizing heaven and Earth are connecting in the here and now. At the base of the Alps, a little girl who used to sing to butterflies was herself undergoing such a transformation too. The butterfly never calls attention to itself or makes noise that forces one to notice. Rather the butterfly is beautiful because God made it, and its essence and beauty come from the change and transformation it has undergone. We all knew we were witnessing something holy and timeless. The purity and innocence of her worship eclipsed a view of herself and always reflected the God who transforms butterflies. That's Wit's worship "style" in a nutshell. Those who had the privilege over the years to see her publicly lead worship never thought, *Oh, she has a nice voice*, but rather were transported to deep reflection on who God was to them in that moment. The sicker she became, the more that truth stood out.

Wit's journey in this life did not include career success or recognition by her peers, even though when she was a teen, we both dreamed one night she won a Dove Award. But everyone who heard her knew she had been graced with intimacy with God, and like a bird, sang to Him continually, regardless of who took notice. Her expression of life through music and poetry showed purposeful surrender and physical humiliations that endeared us to her and drew us closer to the God we could not see. Setback after disappointing setback brought a greater reflection of her loving a God the rest of us couldn't see. It's what set Wit apart. The earthly Wit was disappearing and the new creation was emerging. It felt like God was inviting us to seek Him from behind the curtain of her worship.

We left the Alps for Italy the next day and arrived in Rome. We were in the city with the Roman Colosseum, the Vatican, the Pantheon—and we were walking streets that existed hundreds of years before Jesus was born. The air was brisk and chilly, but not cold, on our first night in Rome. We had no maps and no plan, other than being together, not heading anywhere in particular. The six of us—Darla, Brayden, Heather, Allen, Wit, and I—dipped in and out of the shops and lingered at the famous Spanish steps just a hundred yards from the place we were staying. Not far from the steps we stopped at the famous Trevi Fountain.

Wit and the rest of us threw pennies over our shoulder as is the custom. Over one million dollars are thrown into the fountain and donated to charity every year. The Trevi Fountain (literally meaning three-roads fountain) was originally a critical water source for those living in the area.[53] In those days, the water was also seen as a healing agent or a form of medicine for those who needed it. Legend says there were prophetic water fairies, or nymphs, that delivered healings.[54] Of course, we knew none of that history standing there that evening, staring at its beauty.

Wit tossed one penny over her shoulder, which was supposed to mean you will have a return trip to Rome. We never made it back. As we strolled, Wit and I were able to share in some private conversation, all of it is now firmly anchored in my mind.

"Perhaps destiny is less an event and more a lifetime of divine, ordinary things that form something beautiful in the end," she told me. "Today is enough, Dad. Look around and see His divine beauty in the ordinary." We hugged briefly, and I noted the statements in my mind and heart. She was always wise beyond her years.

Wit's destiny now affects us all and invites us not to use prayer as a penny throwing exercise in futility, but rather to connect with the One who makes all things beautiful in the end. The truth about God, suffering, and faith is that they all intersect at the critical water source of relationship with God. What happens at that intersection is up to us believing and placing our faith on God, not penny throwing, but walking with God on the ordinary days and the sick days too. Faith is not a tool to keep you from suffering but should be your response to the suffering and sorrow that hit your life.

Sorrow and grief change you, but in this darkened place of no understanding there is a deepening and a purifying of your heart and purpose for living. This change has reduced me into unity with God and the friendship of His sufferings. Wit truly understood, like the woman at the well, what it meant to have God's living water, to be satisfied in Him and Him alone. She expresses this in her song "Just One Drop."

There's this living water that's been put in me,
and its filling me up.
Like a spring of water flowing river I've come to find.
Jesus the one who's filled me, I'll never be thirsty again.
You fill me up to the top just one more drop, I'm over flowing
You fill me up to the top just one more drop, I'm over flowing
The well goes deep within, my thirst springs up
Jesus the one who's filled me I'll never be thirsty again.
You fill me up to the top just one more drop, I'm over flowing
You fill me up to the top just one more drop, I'm over flowing
I'm over flowing, I'm over flowing, So let it flow, Let it flow, Let
it flow, I'm letting go, Let it flow. Let it flow, Let it flow, Let it
flow, I'm letting go, Let it flow. I'm overflowing, You just keep
filling me up, God, You just keep filling me up, God.
(repeat)
So let it flow, Let it flow, Let it flow, I'm letting go, Let it flow

Silent, inaudible, discreet, and soundless prayers are now a part of my every day. God is patient with me and waits with me. Sorrow is a place from which no one is exempt and faith does not make one safe. Most at risk in this place, however, is the wrong view of God as the magic fountain of miracles.

When sorrow begins changing your view of God, please don't feel guilty for feeling the way you feel. It's more important to show integrity in processing your pain over the violence or woundedness in your life. One cannot be blinded with sorrow and act as if the eyes of their understanding allow them to see and spew out optimism and sunniness from this darkened place. Shame on those who label themselves Christian and are too busy with their work for God to sit with a friend stuck on the mourning bench beside a tombstone.

The path of this life will have sorrow—we all have this in common. What is not common is to know the God who personally came to walk the path of pain. He did it so that He would experience just what you are. It was not just an act of solidarity with suffering humanity but served to provide resurrection power that would allow us to become new creations and have a life after this one, full of joy and unspeakable beauty.

Wit continually fought for joy and searched for beauty. Wit had the wisdom to know destiny is not a pivotal moment but a collection of the ordinary moments that fill a life. She had the integrity to live out those ordinary moments with authenticity and gratitude. She had the tenacity to keep looking for butterflies and pointing them out to the rest of us, even though we struggled to see.

There is a technique musicians and artist use often, and Wit used it too: it's the art of negative space. The fortissimo is a way a person can write music so that the one playing the notes knows to grow louder and louder. But if music just stayed loud all the time it would lose its dynamic. So the composer also writes in pianissimo to compel the artist to grow very quiet. This was a great breakthrough for composers. It was an emphatic statement allowing a better translation of their work by the one playing the piece. There will be loud and quiet moments on your life's journey. There will be positive events and negative events, but together they form a symphony of God's love. When you are in grief or sorrow, God, although He may not seem to be involved at all, is most likely just allowing for a pianissimo. Don't begrudge the negative space but allow it to be set over your life for emphasizing the faith you have in the God you cannot see.

Wit and I will walk some streets again together only then not limited by time, the dark sorrow driven out by light from the Son. There'll be no sorrow there, and she'll introduce me to the butterfly and the children that went before us. We'll all sit down as a family and share stories and live the dreams of togetherness that are now just dreams. Maybe we'll write a poem or two together. I already have the first line I think: "I lost time once, and I found it in the last place I left it. Wit, it was with you!"

WISDOM MOMENT

The wisdom we seek today is to see others in sorrow too. Talk to someone today about their life and what specific sorrow they may have had to endure. Jot down a few thoughts from that conversation.

INTEGRITY MOMENT

When you read about the *Journal of Nursing Scholarship* studying chronic sorrow, how did it make you feel? Have you met people who suffer with chronic sorrow? List a few ways people could be a friend to someone suffering in this way.

TENACITY MOMENT

Listen to one of these two songs and record your thoughts or emotions after listening.

1. Creedence Clearwater Revival from 1968 called "Have You Ever Seen the Rain"
2. Wit's song "This Path" would also be a good place to feel tenacity at work and you can find it at mikerakes.com.

CHAPTER 7

THE LANGUAGE OF COMPLAINT

Complaining to God means you're already in a relationship with Him.

—Mike Rakes

"What about you, Delmar?" Everett asks. "What are you gonna do with your share of that dough?"

Delmar replies, "I'm gonna visit them foreclosein' son of a guns down at the Indianola Savings and Loan. Slap that money on the barrel head and buy back the family farm. You ain't no kind of man if you ain't got land."[55]

Laughter exploded from the captain's chairs on the second row of our SUV. It was one of the many games Wit came up with for us to play when we were going to be traveling awhile. No "I spy" now that both kids were teens. The game was only won by the person who could keep responding to one quote from the movie with another.

The irreverent movie *O Brother Where Art Thou* is loosely based on Homer's Odyssey. Now, warning to my mom and dad, yes, there is some language in it, but way tamer than the local middle school or the former president of the United States, Donald Trump. If you are religious, do not watch this movie. If you are looking for wholesome entertainment, this is not the pick. There are religious people not living right, sirens, lots of lying to one another, and other things you'll only see otherwise reading the Old Testament.

The main themes of loyalty, surrender, and self-control are reflected in the movie and do allow for some good conversations with your teenagers. The movie opens with a prophecy of a blind prophet over some escaped convicts who are still shackled in chains only moments away from their captors. One of our kids always quoted this line in our friendly family competition, "Fear not the obstacles in your path." Only they would start laughing as they mimicked the pronunciation used by the character in the movie, *obstaakles*. The line is funny, but it's hilarious if you've been in the SUV a little too long. Here's the line in context used by the blind prophet:

> *You seek a great fortune, you three who are now in chains. You will find a fortune, though it will not be the one you seek. But first . . . first you must travel a long and difficult road, a road fraught with peril. Mm-hmm. You shall see thangs, wonderful to tell. You shall see a . . . a cow . . . on the roof of a cotton house, ha. And, oh, so many startlements. I cannot tell you how long this road shall be, but fear not the obstacles in your path, for fate has vouchsafed your reward. Though the road may wind, yea, your hearts grow weary, still shall ye follow them, even unto your salvation.*[56]

There is a bit of parallel I notice, as the prophecy given at the start of the movie fits our lives now. We are in the chains of grief, seeking a great fortune, a reunion. But first we must travel a long and difficult road, fraught with peril. We don't know how long this road shall be, and though the road may wind, and our hearts grow weary, we shall follow even unto our salvation.

For some of my minister friends, this book may feel a little like this irreverent movie. I'm asking uncomfortable questions and pushing on norms that are rarely addressed in Sunday church. Yet, there's this one book in the Bible, Psalms, that carries the same kind of bold realism in it. I can easily feel the pain of the writers and poets in the psalms of lament, which make up one-third of the book. They are priceless to me now, because they tell the truth of what it feels like to be human. Here's a sample:

> O Lord, how long will you forget me? Forever? How long will you look the other way? How long must I struggle with anguish in my soul, with sorrow in my heart every day? How long will my enemy have the upper hand? Turn and answer me, O Lord my God! Restore the sparkle to my eyes, or I will die. Don't let my enemies gloat, saying, "We have defeated him!" Don't let them rejoice at my downfall. But I trust in your unfailing love.[57]

You will probably never find any intellectual satisfaction around understanding the sudden loss of a job or a marriage or the death of someone close to you. The most famous and most awkward lament in the Bible is found in Psalm 88, because there is no answer or resolution. If you are in a rough spot and suffering grief over some loss in your life, you will do well to read the entire passage and take time to feel the pain of the writer.

O Lord, God of my salvation, I cry out to you by day. I come to you at night. Now hear my prayer; listen to my cry . . . My eyes are blinded by my tears. Each day I beg for your help, O Lord; I lift my hands to you for mercy . . . O Lord, I cry out to you. I will keep on pleading day by day . . . I have been sick and close to death since my youth. I stand helpless and desperate before your terrors . . . They swirl around me like floodwaters all day long. They have engulfed me completely. You have taken away my companions and loved ones. Darkness is my closest friend.[58]

If you've never really suffered a loss, you probably skimmed over those Bible verses—like I used to do. Unfortunately, until you're devastated by something, it's so easy to live unaware of what is coming your way. But if you've gone through some bad stuff, the words from Psalm 88 help you to breathe a little easier.

You can hear the pain, but you can also see that the writer is in a deep covenantal relationship with God and that brings with it certain expectations. The speaker doesn't just call out to God in the night; the writer is so desperate that they are moved to cry out during the daytime hours too. The one praying can't understand why God is not responding. A careful paraphrased reading of the text says, "God, You have put me in this spot. God, You are the loser in this overall equation because how can I worship you from the grave?" Like the psalmist who was lamenting, we must develop the art (not formula) of loving God with our whole being. Telling Him when we are disappointed in Him is not a bad thing but a good thing.

The Bible is transparent about the possibility of unanswered prayers. Prayers went unanswered throughout the Bible, and they go unanswered today. God does hear you. Prayer is a conversation between two free parties. God is free to do as He pleases and so are you. The Bible shows that the responsibility of the one praying is to be authentic and respectfully honest, but that does not guarantee an answer. Jesus felt what the psalmist was feeling here when He was in the garden and on the cross. In the end, we must all try to pray for God's will to be done on Earth as it is in heaven.[59] It is an actual act of faith to continue to lament, pray, and worship the God who has allowed your pain.

"Lamenting" is a rarely used religious word that means complaining to God and protesting His lack of engagement on the most critical issues impacting our lives. The passages of lament in the Bible capture the experience of grief and inner pain, and they comfort the broken heart. They let you know God listens and cares. There is no declaration of victory in a lament because the potential for victory has passed, and God has missed it. Silence, sometimes, is not the only truthful response to God when it comes to deep pain; you can also complain or lament while staying truthful, imitate, and devout.

Lament was not a language I had ever spoken to God before; I grew up in church thinking language like this was not only off-limits but might get you struck down by lightning. Lament is telling God how you feel about His action or non-action in the world, usually regarding suffering or injustice. After the second round of Wit's chemo failed and the scan revealed more light-up, there was a whole group of songs Wit could no longer lead the church to sing based on their lack of biblical accuracy, especially if the song guaranteed that God would never let you down.

No one really wants to express that God can still be good and let you down, but it's absolutely true. Those things are not mutually exclusive. Wit and I had many conversations during her suffering years about song writers who can only express what they know to be true but not necessarily encompass the entire spectrum of every person's journey. Some can sing songs in full authenticity because it reflects their understanding and experience with God up to that point in their lives. But others, like Wit, forced to walk a suffering path through this life, must still find a way to be truthful in worship and offer praise to a God they can't fully understand. God does let you down. God doesn't always answer prayer, but we are still deeply and inwardly compelled to worship in spite of our pain. We just have to find the right phrases and lyrics that can deliver our thoughts vocally.

Lamenting is a worship that allows you to be fully authentic about your situation, straight from your heart to God's ear. This kind of suffering worship reveals just how close the person suffering feels to God. They feel close enough to God to express what they are going through, and that is a very good thing. Lamenting, however, is always birthed out of disappointment with God, like the promise of a good friend that is unexpectedly broken. Yet the biblical psalmist who wrote these laments saw themselves in a deeply committed relationship with God. They knew God was not going anywhere, and neither were they. Uncomfortable or not, the air needed to be cleared between them.

Here are some things I wrote in my personal journal to God, which falls into the lamenting category. What my words lack in sophistication they compensate with all-out honesty to the God who not only let me down but has allowed personal devastation to encompass my life and ministry.

> How could God let a young woman who had dedicated
> her life to God since she was small endure such suffering?
> She never partied or went through those rebellious years
> or lived on the wild side. She was our little "Mother Teresa,"
> always caring about others. God, even when diagnosed,
> she saw this challenge as an assignment from heaven and
> took us all on her social media journey to compel us to
> trust you, God, even as her pain, shame, and humiliation
> were so great. Her words, music, and poetry on Instagram

all directed toward you, God, showing her cute, quirky self, keeping the faith. How on your green earth was it too much to ask that you show up and help her or at least ease her suffering at the end?

That is a contemporary modern-day lament. In fact, there may be some sincere people who try to correct me here or see this as a lack of spiritual maturity. Hiding your pain and what you are going through from God and your spiritual family does not equate to spiritual maturity. Lamenting helps one construct a bridge across the gulf of their most intense heart pain and the expectation of a miracle or a promise. I had prayed over her since she was in a bassinet that God would protect her and keep her. Where did those prayers go? Why were they unanswered for our family?

Lamenting to God as a form of prayer helps you endure perplexing new revelations about the God you thought you knew. It lets you endure the forced expansion of your understanding as it relates to God's nature. I now can see sides of God that I had not seen before. Like this from Psalm 6 where the psalmist basically says, "Be nice to me ,God; I'm deteriorating here, God. Heal me because I'm shaking with terror. My entire bed is soaked with tears," and it goes on and on. The writer of Psalm 6 is working out his truth-telling therapy. The God he served let him down. The Psalms teach us that God allows our anger and understands it as part of our humanity, and we need not feel guilty about being cross at God for allowing things to happen in our lives that we do not want.

More than fifty chapters in the Bible carry the voices of people complaining to God when He seems inconsistent and unfair. Well-meaning religious phrases I had used for years could not frame any longer what was happening in my life. Pain forced me to expand my understanding of God. The truth about the wildness of this life, the dangers surrounding our children and us, should not be minimized. Whether you are lamenting or someone you are close to is, allow space for it; don't try to stifle or mitigate it. If you've never experienced that but someone close to you has, allow them to voice it without correcting them. As a form of love and compassion to an angry or suffering neighbor, allow them space to lament. Sometimes listening is love in action. Let's make room for people who have suffered great losses. Listen as a lament develops over coffee without interruption or lecturing as if you have an answer.

Lament is the language of grief that allows you to stay at the table when you are angry about your circumstances and frustrated with God. This keeps God in the equation as you continue the dialogue and relationship you've already had with Him. Honestly, in these dangerous moments, the one Person you don't want to cut out of your life is God. In my case, the only way I could stay at the table was by using lamenting language. I wanted God to hear how I felt about losing Wit and my frustration that He did not speak healing over her. I was learning to stay a faithful follower as my faith faced its greatest threat.

––––––––––––

Where do we go to learn how to cope with devastating losses? To keep our integrity, tell the truth—and not abandon the God we hear about in church that emphasizes overcoming and victory—is very difficult. We can learn all the technical things about grief and loss and have an amazing acumen around the vocabulary of pain. And yet, all that theory won't translate into comfort when you wake up each morning without a loved one. Love and truth telling are the things that keep us at God's table. There is no school to learn to survive loss; your best hope is to be honest about your feelings and use lament when you talk to the Lord.

One important part of my story is that I have a command of the facts when it comes to the study of God and the Bible. But these last six years, four with my daughter battling cancer and two without my daughter, have challenged everything I thought I knew. In some ways, I have had to start my God education over. Lamenting looks hard at the evidence and seeks to tell the truth to God about the suffering. It's in those private times when you realize that as an American Christian, suffering never seemed like a possibility.

The commonness of human sorrow, grief, and trauma invites you into the process of either walking away from God disappointed or digging deeper until you uncover a more authentic faith in this time and place. The undisclosed pain my family has suffered beyond the obvious is the bewilderment around the apparent inactivity of God when we needed Him most. Frankly, it matters, because to get the foundation of our beliefs in alignment with the bigger story of Scripture, we must understand we are blaming God for withholding things He never promised to give us.

The depth of my loyalty to God now after our loss is greater, though my past passionate love for God in this moment seems far away and, if I'm totally honest, incredibly shallow. The depth of my love for Whitney forces me to tell the truth about what happened and offer the unanswered questions as an invitation for you to develop a deeper covenant with God, realizing that you will suffer hard and difficult things in this life too.

Can you imagine following Jesus your whole life and then entering a season of suffering and just blocking Him out because the pain is too much? How much more painful that would be for some devout person of faith! Your faith does not and cannot stay the same during and after seasons of suffering. It is through lamenting that you invite God into that process of your faith evolving. By trying to grin and bear it alone, you find yourself distant from the God of your old faith and His silence becomes all you know of Him. Lament breaks the silence as a broken heart finds a way to talk with God again. Lamenting is a genuine part of a healthy grieving process and often brings you to trust God again in spirit and truthfulness. The process of lament allows you to complain, weep, and worship with authenticity and helps maintain your sanity.

God came to us in our human condition and experienced all things like us. Even the shortest verse in the Bible, "Jesus wept,"[60] takes on new meaning and significance. Sitting in the disappointment of unanswered prayer is a great way to resist the devil that speaks horrible things into the mind during times of loss. Lamenting is sitting in the ashes of disappointment and waiting for strength to move forward. Job did that very thing in his day. It is a respectful way to complain to God about all your unmet expectations and the perplexing nature of His action or non-action.

The wounds from our loss are dense with varying degrees of intensity. Although we are not far into life without Wit, I can already tell that time won't heal us. I am confident that the rawness of my emotion and vocabulary will fade overtime, and so, where the sharpness of that stands out in my words, I ask for grace and prayer. But friends who have not suffered severe losses need to know that a person with an everyday kind of faith will be severely impacted by various traumas and pain. Who wants to talk about a question like, how can a loving God stand by and seemingly do nothing to ease the pain of a devout worshiper or stop the death-train altogether from making a stop at the house of a 27-year-old? How does the mind and heart recover after watching four long years of hair loss, no-hope reports, and plaguing physical pain so entwined with our precious daughter's memories that it feels like we can't let go of the one for fear we will lose the other?

For our family, there will never be any intellectual satisfaction around understanding Wit's premature death. To imagine no holidays, no more worship leading, and no grandchildren from her pushes the boundaries of our spiritual and emotional strength. I never thought God would allow something like this to happen to me, to us. Grief is like setting a wild, kicking donkey loose in your living room; there's no coaxing it out the door, and it damages everything that you value.

I have several Black friends who are pastors, and they texted me on the first anniversary of Wit's death. They said they were thinking of Darla and me. The only reason I share they were Black is because only one white pastor-friend texted me. Truth be told, I've never texted a minister friend on a one-year anniversary after his or her loss. However, my friends of color lament well because it's a part of their stories as they experience the trauma of implicit and explicit racism. It's that suffering and pain that informs their daily ministries. We must learn to lament in deeply honest ways and bring our sorrows and wounds and griefs to God. This opens the greater revelation of God's nature among us, both His suffering and His companionship in our troubles. It is our suffering that allows us to enter someone else's pain and offer camaraderie.

Lamenting allows the soul to find a way to trust God even in the darkest night. Worship after loss is being fully present in the pain and keeping the conversation open between God and you. God has let me down, a lot. That's a statement of lament. Some shy away from this language, but those who are in a heart covenant with God never fear honesty or truth telling. God will probably, at some point on your journey, let you down too. But these things are not God's fault, rather our shallow understandings. The lament language allows the heart to be angry at God respectfully and offer it up as authentic worship. God already knows how you feel, so hiding it doesn't make it disappear. Lament language helps to offer even the deepest pains in your life as worship.

Like the psalmist, I am in a covenant with God too. I expected Him to give me a long life with my daughter. I expected to hold her kids and have them over for Thanksgiving and birthdays, but that will never happen. Did God do that? Did cancer do that? No matter what linguistic spin you want to put on things, God has permitted my heart to bear this unspeakable pain. A person in a deep relationship with God will sometimes express anger or disappointment precisely because they are already in a relationship with God, and they know the relationship is strong enough to bear the weight of disappointment and sorrow.

Lament is the language of grief that seeks to not abandon God but keep Him in the equation. Lament fills the awkward silence between a broken heart and the God who is beyond understanding. Lament is the grieving person's way of trusting and remaining truthful. Lament allows one to complain, weep, and worship with authenticity. Lament gives voice to the deepest thoughts in the soul of a broken heart. Lament is sitting in the ashes of disappointment, what was lost—or never was—and waiting for God to respond. Lament keeps you connected to God in the darkest night.

When Wit was a toddler, we would take her on rides around the neighborhood in the little red wagon, with her brother riding his bike in large, looping circles around us. It was always amazing to me that she would sit looking backward out of the wagon—like in the old days, when a princess would ride in the carriage with her back to the driver. She was less concerned about what was coming up next in the future and more concerned with living in the now, taking it all in.

Some people live in debt to time. They talk about "time getting away from them" or "time going by," but in the spirit realm, time is a human invention of trying to predict how things go. Things run on seasons, a time for this and a time for that, a linear construct to help us try to predict how much time we have left—or how much time until we get married, get that promotion, or finally feel happy.

But Wit didn't live that way. Like a princess riding backward in her horse-drawn carriage, taking in the full view of the world and all its nature, Wit lived outside of time it seemed. Even with a terminal diagnosis, she did not live as though time was constrained or limited. We suffer now in this moment because time feels like a big heavy chain. My ambition has evaporated as some human ego invention and my calling is to live wide awake to my wife, my son and his wife, and my grandkids. To help people every day to live less distracted and more awake. To compel people to "do good" every day and do it all in the name of Christ. In this way, I can live and breathe and fight for joy every day.

Wit taught me, in this life's carriage, when we don't know where we are going, to slow down, be fully present, and take in the view. No more time, just the endless beginning of a new song. Wit showed us the wisdom in being okay and realizing that none of us are driving our own carriages. Wit had an integrity in her inner life, a holy place where she retreated often. When time stopped for her, when Jesus called her to the reality where time and suffering ceased, we bore witness to the passing of a life lived fully surrendered—a life lived full of tenacity—from the time-ridden, decaying world into an eternity we long for.

WISDOM MOMENT

Pray that God would help you notice and listen to people who have been disappointed with God. What emotion are you aware of when you read, "Lament is telling God how you feel about His action or non-action in the world"?

INTEGRITY MOMENT

Take a blank index card and or a page in your journal and write a personal lament to God if you have one. Complete the following sentence, and then add your own thoughts and feelings.

God, I was disappointed when You did not...

TENACITY MOMENT

Write a prayer to God and include a sentence or two using the word "lament."

CHAPTER 8
IN THE QUESTIONING

Anyone can become angry—that is easy; but to be angry with the right person, and to the right degree, and at the right time, and for the right purpose, and in the right way—that is not within everybody's power and is not easy.[61]

—Aristotle

"Princess Krystle goes into the dark woods to look for little lost girls who are alone," Wit said. "They must find their path through the forest to the Great King." She and I were writing our first book together after dinner the day Wit started kindergarten. We used crayons. The book was never published, and in all transparency, it was only a few pages long. It was about Krystle (spelling by Wit), a princess "more beautiful on the inside than the outside." She borrowed the phrase her mom used with her all the time.

Princess Krystle, after a few adventures, would find her way to the king. It is such a great story with extraordinary meaning for me now. This book is our second written together with the same theme. Our princess, Wit, goes into the dark forest of suffering, looking for individuals who are lost, jaded, confused, or shamed; helps them endure the dragon's lies and discouragement; and fights the dragon off through worship, finding strength to endure the battle using wisdom, integrity, and tenacity. Princesses always defeat dragons if their fathers are the king!

Legends, fairy tales, and the Bible all have one thing in common: dragons. The very first book of the Bible in the first chapter and twenty first verse says in the original Hebrew that God created *tannin* or "sea-monster" or "dragon" as it's translated. [62] *Tannin* is such a powerful creature that Job 7:12 says it needed a "guard" to keep it under control.

About 600 years before Mary and Joseph came to Bethlehem in the city of David, their ancestors had been taken captive to a metropolitan city called Babylon. The ancient ruins of Babylon are believed to be in southern Iraq. King David's descendants were taken captive to Babylon and surrounded by the sights, sounds, and songs of other religions. One of the gods they worshiped there passionately was Marduk.

Their legend about Marduk demanded a great parade and celebration because he had killed the great sea dragon Tiamat. [63] The myth says he split the dragon in half and set up guards to watch each half to keep it from coming back to life. [64] There, Marduk created a heavenly temple for the people to dwell on Earth with the gods. The people of Babylon would have annual events celebrating Marduk the dragon slayer. Children would replay the battle scene on the streets, songs were written to celebrate the legend, and the worship and noise coming from the festival each year would be deafening. [65]

The only-one-God people—the descendants of David and the ancestors of Mary and Joseph—were surrounded by these celebrations and songs, which must have confused the children growing up in captivity because they had been taught that the truly most powerful King and only God was the God of Moses, Abraham, Isaac, and Jacob. I can almost hear their questions: "Daddy, why are they celebrating Marduk? I thought *we* served the most powerful God?"

Isaiah 27:1 says, "In that day the Lord will take his terrible, swift sword and…He will kill the dragon" (NLT). This promise from two hundred years earlier confirmed that, indeed, the God of the Israelites is the One who slays dragons. And although they were held captive and had to listen to those songs praising Marduk year after year, the parents would sing the psalms and tell the stories of prophets to declare the greatness of their God, even if they did not see or feel His greatness in their captivity.

A dragon called cancer attacked our innocent princess on her journey through life's dark forest. Those four years were like watching the taunting celebrations of a pagan tribe, much like those dads raising daughters in captivity. Each negative report—month after month and year after year—rubbed our noses in our unanswered prayers. The dragon traumatized our daughter as she underwent various tests and treatments. The stark reality that our princess was moving deeper into the dark woods never to return to us the same made us feel like the taunts were accurate. The pain was like a bone marrow aspiration, where a liquid marrow sample is taken through a hollow needle to examine the deepest core sample from a person's blood—a ten on anyone's pain scale. Yet, the battle was to endure however long her life span and make it all the way to the King. She did.

From the outset, we knew Wit's prognosis was horrible and it continued to worsen over time. But no matter, that would just be part of the greater story we thought. Wit would be an ambassador of the King for her generation and one day tell of how He slayed the cancer dragon in her life. We expected God to protect her and rescue her according to the story we were writing.

It's important to know that our Father is a King who watches over us in our journeys, but watching over us, as Wit's story shows, is very different from protecting us. We learned through our time in the dark forest that no one generation—sixth-century BC or ours—is allowed to approach the Scriptures randomly; the words in the sacred text are to help each generation navigate the dark forest and our battles with the dragons we face. The ultimate dragon of death has been banished from the King's presence forever, and after you make it through the dark forest, all the tears are wiped away, which must mean our traumas and memories are healed there too. To leave this life is to be present in the next with the King. The ultimate dragon of death has already been defeated and so death has lost its sting. Wit never ceased to exist and is now present with the King. But trouble will still come in this world, and those of us left behind in the dark forest still have dragons we must face.

Now I'm in the dark woods of grief and the dragon of why presents himself to me continually. When facing the Why dragon, the question becomes this: Can we believe the King loves us and not abandon our loyalty regardless of the severity of our torture through the dark woods of life?

Why did God let Wit die? There, I've said it! That's what swirls in the mind of a father when a loss like Wit's defies explanation. I hate death. I hate that people must die. I hate all forms of suffering, but I hate death the most. I hate the lasting affect it has on the living. Some years ago, I officiated a funeral for a ninety-two-year-old saint. She was so vibrant, healthy, and active that her family was shocked by her death. They wept like I would have never expected at her passing. Loss and grief should never be minimized, and I didn't minimize theirs. But the emotional drama present in the family over her loss was a little unnerving for me at the time on several levels. I hope you don't think poorly of me for this, but ninety-two? Was someone here expecting a different outcome? Our loss was at twenty-seven. Please give me a little grace here. We would have taken thirty-two. Forty-two. Fifty-two. Sixty-two. Seventy-two. But ninety-two? Why don't we do a happy dance for all the decades of life and health she enjoyed? And why didn't Wit get those decades too?

The difficulties we experience in life create the choices that become our personal stories. There are incidents along the way that reveal our character and progress toward reaching our destiny. All of us have things we expect out of life, but those expectations won't be our story. Our story will come from the way life really goes. I had a specific story in my head: I would see my kids grow older into their forties and fifties, and then I would die before them. I saw Darla and myself retiring and hosting our kids' kids on holidays, but life didn't go as I expected.

Now my story, like it or not, is how I respond to my crushed expectations. The old sometimes have to bury the young. Here's the thing: whenever you see grandparents attending a funeral in the family, something has gone terribly wrong. The "supposed tos" of our life stories aren't guaranteed. Living morally, eating clean, and doing good are still no contract that life will go as you plan. If life doesn't go as planned, and if there is a premature death, it would only be natural to ask, "Why?"

My freshman year at college, only seventeen, I heard the professor talking about Socrates' recommendation to investigate things that did not make sense with questions. The questions look for the contradictions and use a few steps to uncover true knowledge about the situation. We call it the Socratic method. When difficulties arise in your own personal story, you must have perspective and wisdom to be able to keep navigating toward your destination. Asking why can be a bridge to help you cross the Grand Canyon of unmet expectations.

My heart was racing like coming out of a bad dream when I could not remember Wit's sixteenth birthday party—for a few minutes, I couldn't think of what we did for her. After a little while it started to come back in bits and pieces as I obsessed over not losing any memories of her at all. "She looked so grown up on that day," my journal records. Mature beyond her years, self-composed, not given to emotional outbursts or breakdowns. She always carried her five-foot-three self as if she were much older. Yet because she took time for children anywhere and everywhere, it was easy to think of her as a kid too, but she wasn't. That morning she smiled as she worked with her mom in the kitchen, to prepare the gluten-free birthday cake and other food for the small number of friends coming over to celebrate her.

Months before her sixteenth birthday, Wit and I snuck out of the house to go do some practice driving preparing for her upcoming driver's test. Standing on the top stair leading into the garage from the laundry room, we were faced with our first choice.

> *"I recommend my SUV over your mom's compact BMW,"*
> *I said. "If you learn to drive in a huge vehicle, learn to*
> *control it and park it, then you can easily pass the driving school test in a smaller vehicle when the time comes."*

We went to pick up some coffee before going to a church parking lot for our very first driving experience together. Sitting in the drive-through line, she suggested we pick a different church parking lot other than our home church so that no one would recognize her, so we decided on a large Baptist church. She seemed nervous, hardly sipping on her tall London Fog tea. Wearing a thick distressed sweatshirt from Urban Outfitters, she adjusted the seat to fit her small frame and short legs. I talked her through the one-foot-only driving method, and she rested her left sneaker against the door. After some instruction, she quickly picked up on how to drive the Chevy Tahoe.

I was blown away by how dialed into my voice she was, but soon she was navigating her way around the obstacles while nervously making small talk with me. Though she didn't need it, we took three more Saturdays grabbing coffee and tea on our way to just ride around the church parking lot. I wish now we had added a few more Saturdays. She was so proud of herself when she passed her test easily, and I was too.

Wisdom comes to us this same way. Our stories take a difficult twist, and we are forced into larger situations than we are currently prepared to handle. We are forced to navigate the dark forest in large SUVs. Sometimes people say, "God doesn't put more on us than we can bear!" Well, that's not in the Bible and it's also not true. They are referring to the first letter Paul wrote to the Corinthians, but the verse in question has to do with temptations and not life's suffering and difficulties.[66] These are usually the same people who say, "If God closes a door, He will open a window!" That is not a promise; it is a projection. Understandably, the people who use those phrases want to believe God will never keep them from getting what they want. But it is not truth. We have no control over the God of mystery and this puzzling house with endless doors and windows. Trust me, when God closes a door, He's not opening a window to let you squeeze out. And He might even slam the door rather than close it gently.

Nearly all the men and women written about in the Bible faced overwhelming setbacks, trouble, and pain. They knew a God who often closed the door on their comfort. I think life often hits us with things way beyond our ability to handle, and God seems to permit it. Wisdom comes through your trouble, not from a book or class lecture. Gaining wisdom or coming to wisdom means you're in over your head. It also means God is not letting you have things the way you want them.

When you go to the movies, you're literally paying money to see how the protagonist reacts and responds to all the hell thrown at them by the antagonist. Can they become a better person after all they experience? Wit's life was no fairy tale, but she ended up responding to all the darkness of hell thrown at her with wisdom, integrity, or tenacity on any given day. You won't know who you are until all hell breaks out in your life and you are given a chance to respond.

Personally, I've been battling the intellectual dragon named Why since Wit died. I label something a dragon if its purpose is to steal your faith and block your growth as a person or in taking a next step toward your destiny. Dragons are always dangerous, unless it's a Disney movie of course, then only moderately so. You've met the Why dragon too if you lost someone to an unexpected death, a sudden and violent accident, or a horrible crime. Sunday church dignity won't help with fire-breathing dragons. No, the only thing that defeats a dragon is bringing your questions honestly before God. Asking why only hinders your faith if you do not want to listen for an answer or if your questions sound more like a bitter curse than a desperate prayer. You are not a better Christian for refusing to ask God why! The Bible even says in the book of James, "If you need wisdom, ask our generous God, and he will give it to you. He will not rebuke you for asking."[67] Wisdom comes from asking the right question, to the right person, in the right way, at the right time, to gain the right perspective. For me, God was the best One to ask and receive help from on this quest.

Some people don't have to ask why. I'm not sure if Wit asked why, not very often at least. Her journals don't seem to indicate it. But those of us who do have to ask why must be open to not getting a satisfactory answer or to getting no answer at all. What you really desire is wisdom, not necessarily an explanation. However, to become obsessed with the why is not good either. Why is a pretty unforgiving place to try to live.

The dragon and the princess story will play out in your life, and you must learn to hold the tension of knowing that the King has the power to do anything along with the understanding that we are invited to share in His sufferings. Americans—for the past four decades at least, dating all the way back to the inception of the American dream—have believed they are able to circumvent the valleys of life and live from mountain top to mountain top because they are a "King's kid." The assumption is that those who suffer must have done something wrong or left the proverbial door open to evil. American Christians almost always attach sin to suffering. The subtler abuse of that false belief is that those who are not suffering are in this position because they kept the moral code and were generous in their donations. In this belief, we commoditize God; it's as if we say, "God, I'll keep Your law if You bless me and keep the dragons away." It's a transactional, *quid pro quo* kind of spirituality. In other words, this belief wrongly says we need God for safety and protection because we get something out of it; we don't serve Him out of a sense of loyalty, love, and gratitude.

God modeled for us how to carry our sorrows, knowing that just on the other side of the dark forest is a full and eternal life with the King. We do have resurrection life here and now, and He didn't say, "If you'll do certain things for me or act in certain ways, then you won't have trouble." It goes without saying that much human suffering comes upon a person through choices and decisions they make. However, we must be careful not to throw those who have experienced sexual abuse, live with disabilities, have chronic diseases, had tragic accidents, or have a myriad of other maladies—even cancer—into the same categories. Christians should not shame or blame victims. God does promise we can face our pain, overcome our troubles, and keep our faith, not because of what we do, but because He's with us to help us endure.

Soon after Wit passed, many cautioned us to "never ask God why." To which my internal response was always, "Why?" Coming to wisdom is a messy and often-irreverent process; just ask any college professor who teaches freshmen. And it is okay that grief is not as clean and tidy as you might think. Trey Gowdy's book *Doesn't Hurt to Ask* helped frame my questions in a more authentic and respectful way. Trey, a former prosecutor, showed how critical the why question is when you are digging for the truth:

"Why" can mitigate a killing from murder to self-defense. ... "Why" is in many instances the question that matters most and the question that matters least; it just depends on the instance and the particular facts. ... In murder cases, "why" almost never matters except in self-defense cases. ... But you can rest assured that it is the first question the jury has in both their individual and collective minds. People want to know why things happen.[68]

Why did God not keep Whitney from dying? There are many why questions we have as a family. Science doesn't even know how one gets this disease. No one in our immediate family ever had cancer. Just this morning, I heard about a colleague's son—who's only one year older than Wit—who found a lump on his neck. None of the treatments could save him, and he lived fifteen months after his diagnosis. There was no cancer in the family tree, healthy vegetarians only, and now their family of four has been destroyed by the loss. The hard truth is, the researchers can't even answer why. The medical doctors do not know why. They know the age range and gender that this cancer shows up but not why. They know the odds of surviving this cancer of the blood but not why people get it.

It goes against the deepest parts of our human nature not to ask why. Children ask why all the time. That's how they learn. It's the question that develops in young children as they begin to reason and connect the dots to see how the world makes sense. Aren't we all God's children? Did not Jesus' own words tell us to come to Him as little children? Whoever gave that advice may have forgotten that one-third of all the psalms are complaints to God about why He did or did not do a particular thing.

Why can be a dangerous dragon or a path to wisdom. There is a right way to ask the why question and a wrong way. Throughout those four long years for our family, the question was more central to our lives and vocation. Why was God staying silent? Why was there no movement of the miraculous? Since science could not slay the Why dragon, surely God could. Gowdy displays in his book how you can ask the why question and essentially provide the answer you already think is true in the question itself. Here are a few honest questions to God from my journal that I never intended to publish.

- *Isn't it true that You say in the Bible that "no weapon formed against you shall prosper"?*[69]
- *Don't You say in Psalm 91 that if we abide under the shadow of the Almighty, we will be safe from pestilence and disease?*
- *You healed someone in the Gospels by using mud; could You not have at least helped the immunotherapy work?*
- *Since young women Wit's age all over the world squander their physical and spiritual futures chasing fun and pleasure and live long lives, then is the statement that "only the good die young" accurate?*
- *Is it true that the Bible says that if children obey their parents in the Lord, they will have long lives on the earth?*[70]
- *Why didn't You stop her from getting cancer in the first place?*
- *Did I waste my time praying over her every night since You gave her to us?*
- *Why didn't any healing Bible verses that work for other people work for us?*
- *Why did You allow her lungs to collapse while she was in front of the whole church leading worship?*

God is not a Sunday morning hobby for Darla, Brayden, Heather, and me, and "wisdom" is not just a vocabulary word. My calling has always been to be an ambassador representing God to others. However, as you can see from the way my pain and false assumptions crafted the questions, there is no wisdom to be found from an insufficient understanding or misunderstanding of the Scriptures. In this dead-end scenario, with the Creator of the universe the loop of questions takes me nowhere, because they've already predetermined the answers based on misappropriated facts. There's nothing constructive in this process. My questions were providing some answers though; I was angry and disappointed with the God who I thought would save my daughter. These questions blocked my faith, the dragon blocking my path to the King.

Questions can rotate through our minds daily and be more like tornadoes than just stormy winds. Questions can move in our minds like a vicious circle, always bringing us back to the place we started. To a person who has never lost someone, questions like those may seem frightening. For someone who's never been face to face with a fire-breathing dragon, hell bent on destroying their faith—I can understand the reticence. Reading questions like that can certainly make you uncomfortable, especially when hearing them expressed by a friend out loud at a coffee shop. But as J. R. R Tolkien said, "It does not do to leave a live dragon out of your calculations, if you live near him."[71] Only wisdom can help with Why dragons.

Wisdom is what helps us reframe these questions so we don't let the Why dragon get the best of us. Here are some better questions that I think get me closer to God's promise for wisdom.

- *Isn't the way some dedicated Christians try to pin God down to certain verses in the Bible constructing a God in their own image?*
- *Isn't it true that the reason we decree and declare robotic recitations of healing Bible verses because we are trying to control God and get the outcome we want?*
- *Isn't it a fact that American Christianity is about believing that having to suffer or live in varying levels of discomfort is not biblical?*

- *Is it possible that some well-meaning people, not trained in Bible interpretation, misrepresent certain passages on divine healing?*
- *Do we fight our so-called "spiritual/physical battles" based on believing we never have to identify with the sufferings of Jesus on the cross?*
- *Isn't it true that the belief "Jesus suffered so I don't have to" is more a privileged American way of looking at the gospel than it is global?*
- *Why are people of faith, who are in deep relationship and covenant with God, so afraid to ask why?*

The truth is, I may not have exactly the right questions here, but I am still at God's table in covenant relationship with Him. When I see Wit's number at the top of my speed dial, I often think of our close dad and daughter relationship. Cancer cheated her out of having babies and cheated me out of having more time with her. I keep her number on the phone because she's not forgettable. Some days, missing her triggers something deep within. Her dying is an injustice and not fair, but putting God on trial for her death is foolishness. You don't recover from grief, but gaining wisdom helps you put it in the right context. No one recovers from losses like this, but we learn to adjust our expectations and lives to adapt.

Wit died on our parental watch, under God's oversight, but she did not die because we didn't pray hard enough or believe with all our hearts. You name it, we tried it. The wisdom I offer you—after walking through all these hope-filled and expensive faith iterations—is that it's possible for you to suffer in this life; whether you believe that truth will ultimately be irrelevant. The superior question is, will you seek God's wisdom to help you when you do suffer? Your life is a story; there will be many difficulties, and maybe even tragedies, along the way for which you will need great wisdom.

I am the first to admit I deserve nothing from God, so let's get that on record. God owes me nothing. I am to be a humble bond servant, enduring whatever afflictions are allowed to overwhelm my life. But I am a father, who has passionately pursued God from the time I was very young. For four decades I've sought after God every day, up many hours before dawn seeking to "know" God. God knows I say this for your benefit, not my own. God is not a *quid pro quo* God. There is no such thing as a transactional God. Wisdom helps you leave the mathematical section of the library and head over to the mystery aisle where dragons live. God will do or not do as He pleases. And you'll have to learn to live with that reality. He is not about to be controlled by the likes of me or you.

Messy questions are far from sacrilege, irreverence, or blasphemy. For the grieving or the terminally ill, life will not feel orderly when you must get up every morning with a death-fog obscuring your path. For me, wisdom was attempting to reconcile my understanding of God's personal love for me while trying not to throw up as I thought about Wit's passing. These are the things that make religious people uncomfortable. This is why well-meaning people tell a devastated, brokenhearted person full of love and longing for their loved one not to ask why.

In an essay in the book *Heuristics and Biases: The Psychology of Intuitive Judgment*, authors Amos Tversky and Daniel Kahneman studied mystery under a microscope and found that "uncertainty is an unavoidable aspect of the human condition."[72] Well, thanks for reminding us that this life has far more questions than answers contained within it. Other intelligent people from other centuries—like Camus, Dostoevsky, and Milan Kundera—all framed this mystery in ways that make even the strongest follower of Jesus slump their shoulders. They framed suffering as absurd, wretched, and banal. The loss of meaning in relation to suffering is the thread that ties these authors together.[73]

There is a mystery to birth, life, and death that does not lend itself to simple and finite human resolutions—and certainly not contemporary American Christianity. I am not able to answer why you are going through what you are going through. I don't know why my daughter had to die. I don't enjoy seeing other people's Thanksgiving tables full of grandkids on Instagram. I would not wish our experience on anyone, but this horror is not how I expected my life to play out. And now that I've put it all down in writing for you, the questions that lead nowhere are obvious.

Wisdom helps us see that prayer should never be viewed as an automatic way to get a miraculous rescue. Prayer is a reaching out to and into God, humbly asking for intervention and wisdom. You will most definitely need one or the other. Neither lying flat on my face, crying, humbly asking God to stop Wit's blood cancer in private or at other times "going boldly before the throne" in loud, confident tones did anything to change Wit's outcome. It didn't take Wit's suffering away either. Praying, "Don't allow this cup of death to be forced down our throats," is a painful lament when your daughter is across town, suffering both day and night.

As the years rolled by, the prayers became more desperate. Reminding ourselves of Bible stories—like the persistent widow in the Gospels who would not let go and got what she wanted—only heightened our faith and energy. The widow got what she asked for, and we did not. You can't write a vulnerable section like this and not run the risk of people thinking, *Well, you didn't pray with the right heart or attitude*, or *You didn't stand on the Word*, or *Your motive must have been wrong in praying for a miracle*. All I will say is, keep this book handy after your prayers end up at the wailing wall.

I now take my place with other believers around the world who have been thrown not only into a furnace of great pain but also of holy fire. Frankly, I think it would be rare to find someone with great faith who had never persevered through the fires of disappointment and unanswered prayer with God. We still are more like Socrates, Plato, and Aristotle in our thinking, searching for logic and reasoning, as if life is a ladder to climb. But God is Spirit, mystery, and love; we enter His presence here and now in our pain, questions, and even in our sorrow as we seek wisdom and strength for this day.

Even the bad questions reveal arrogant assumptions about how the God of heaven works in our world. They expose a subculture of charismatic arrogance, where we believe we know how God works and that we know how to get God to do what we believe is His will. We think we know how prayer and faith work, but we don't. It's a mystery. It is in God's nature to heal. It is also in God's nature not to. Go figure. We know God is making all things new, but we don't know exactly how He is doing that or what that means for life on Earth.

Wit was made new, and now I am continually being made new. Because the old Wit is forever gone, the old Mike is forever gone too. Although we physically live in separate locations for this time-torn moment—she on the side of "no time" and me still stuck in time—we are forever bonded. So, going after wisdom about your situation means you must start from where you are, even if you ask bad questions at first. Look to gain God's perspective on your situation, including what's next. Slaying the Why dragon and gaining wisdom means going directly to the Source of everything—not to learn how to not ask why, but to learn how to humbly ask why in a way that draws you closer to Him. To get back to the Author and Origin of everything. To go organic.

———————

"Happy sixteenth birthday from your mom and me," I said as I handed her the keys to a Honda Fit. She hugged me tightly with her short arms, only making it about halfway around her big dad. The next Saturday, she drove us to a local farmers' market. We ordered coffee on the way, stopping at a drive-through, ordering a grande cappuccino for Mom, an iced venti Americana for me, and a tall Earl Grey tea for Wit. We strolled through the market of dull-colored carrots with dangly roots at the bottom and bundles of Romaine lettuce. Darla and Wit filled a few small cloth bags with our veggies for the week and purchased a large bundle of fresh peonies.

Wit was the passionate farm-to-fork person in our family, and it wasn't a pastime for her; it was a lifestyle. It may sound a little corny to you, but she wanted to do things God's way in every dimension of her life. Farm to table is more than a modifier describing a restaurant that uses more natural ingredients. It's a movement that essentially helps people who are done with processed goods get back to the literal roots of our food. Getting to wisdom is much the same; it takes going back to the basics of belief and faith.

We were all tormented about allowing experts to try to poison cancer out of her with chemo. We knew of many who had tried to go against terminal cancer with faith alone, and only knew personally of one successful case thirty years prior. We are a family that believes in supernatural healing *and* believe God is One who gives knowledge to scientists. Faith and science are not in opposition, and that kind of thinking, in my opinion, is dangerously misguided. The most important theologian a few hundred years after Jesus, Origen, wrote, "For those who are adorned with religion use physicians as servants of God, knowing that He himself gave medical knowledge to men, just as He himself assigned both herbs and other things to grow on the earth."[74] It's not anti-faith or unbiblical to depend on brilliant people to use their God-given gifts to bless the world—even if it's medicine, it's actually wisdom.

For the most part, the way people thought about farming and all its instruments did not change much until agriculture shifted from growing what you and your family needed to eat to making money off it. The shift from hand labor to the table to the more progressive inventions and building of giant machines to mass-produce food took place after the Civil War. Food became big business, and it greatly affected the ingredients and the quality of the food.

In that same way, spirituality has been lost in some congregations as the ingredients to faith have changed and the quality of our faith has diminished in some ways. Regardless of whether you go to a large church or a small church, you will have to take personal responsibility for what you do with what you learn from your faith community.

To get to wisdom, you will have to engage with God using personal spiritual practices. To show up once a week and listen to a message is like eating processed food: at some point it will become evident. Wisdom never was and never will be delivered in one tidy box of answers for suffering, pain, and trouble. Yet, the loss of organic spirituality will become detrimental to your overall spiritual connection between the God who cares for you and your ability to receive (eat) that into your spiritual system. How easy it is to blame a God who is only known through Sunday messages. No amount of great messaging can carry an entire family experiencing opioid addiction, mental illness, or cancer, and it certainly can't help with overwhelming grief. You must have wisdom to spiritually survive all the bad things that will hit you in this life.

We have experienced the full range of emotions about Wit dying, from anger to confusion, but putting God on trial for her death is at best foolishness and at worst even demonic in inspiration. When you find yourself in times of great suffering, the most important questions I have to offer you are: Will you seek God's wisdom to help you when you are suffering? Are you willing to let God be the healer and you the humble seeker? Are you good with whatever He chooses to do or not do? Wit and I are asking that you be open to praying for the grace to deal with all you are going through because we know God does care for you and that Jesus cautioned us that this life would be hard and full of trouble.

Wisdom understands that suffering levels the ground upon which we all travel. Biblical wisdom helps me see God as the Healer. Wisdom says I am to be the humble seeker. Wisdom can be found for suffering and grieving hearts by understanding and living in the bigger story of God. Wit had the wisdom to know there is power in your pain and you must endure it like a good soldier. Through her integrity, she showed that believing for your miracle the whole time is what you should do. She had the tenacity to step into her pain every day with confidence because she was all in, in this deep relationship with God, no matter how bad things got.

Wisdom shows me that death is not final but is the passage into the new creation Jesus provided for us here and now. Push in and ask the hard questions, lightning won't strike you down. Do you remember Jesus allowing the little children to come to Him? Jesus taught His disciples that, unless you come as one of these little ones, you won't enter the kingdom of heaven.[75]

One way the church can look more like its Founder is to stop shaming those who suffer or lose people to suicide or cancer and allow room for mystery and no answers. Suffering changes everyone in the family. Suffering often makes you unrecognizable to yourself. Once you've lost everything, the temporary things matter less; only what will last into the next reality matters.

Princess Wit taught me how to defeat the dragons of life with faith and wisdom. Real faith will always cost you everything because it's the very thing you stake your life on. Faith demands an integration into all the dimensions of your life, even the hidden parts. Especially the times in life when you have no answers or when your faith is most exposed. It is easy to believe you are a person of faith when you get everything you're praying for, and all of your kids are still alive, and the suffering truck has made no deliveries on your street. I wish nothing bad for you, but I am coming to see that everyone suffers. This is the one thing of which I am confident. Faith is not a tool to be used to get what you want, and it certainly can't be quantified. Faith is your breath; it's this breathing in and out as you walk through the dark woods of your life.

Wit's story points us all to see God as the great King over the dark forest. We are just as close to Him, breathing in and out during the most intense battles in the forest, as if we were worshiping Him in the next reality. This is the wisdom Wit offered to me through her journal. She wrote, "He is great, and His love for us non-negotiable and our opportunity, this divine invitation, is to know Him and experience Him here and now, as we little by little make our way." All of our lives pass through the dark forest, but the King is overseeing our exit from the forest and into the great city that will exceed all our expectations. It will be the land of no whys!

WISDOM MOMENT

List three of your personal spiritual practices—things you do or ways you seek to be present with God—that you do each month.

INTEGRITY MOMENT

Think about a time when you were filled with uncertainty over something very important. If it was resolved, how long did it take to get resolution? If it was not resolved and you're still experiencing uncertainty over something, explore the idea by journaling a few paragraphs about it.

TENACITY MOMENT

When you were reading the questions I wrote in this chapter, did you feel comfortable or uncomfortable with what I asked? Take some time to think through why you felt the way you did. Perhaps take some time to write out some questions of your own.

PART III
INTO THE MYSTERY

CHAPTER 9
LETTING GO
OF CERTAINTY

There is an excruciating anguish that comes from watching a loved one suffer and being struck with an inarticulate silence.

—Mike Rakes

A just-turned-three Wit came run-skipping toward the very large pool that summer on vacation, and I remember the pink bathing suit with the little, fluffy skirt around her midsection offset by the obnoxious floaties inflated on each arm. She ran to the side of the pool and jumped into my arms as her brother swam all around us like a fish. Her mom came in the pool behind her. Water forms in my eyes as I reveal this part of our lives because we were perfect. Just the four of us. Parents in their thirties with hopes and dreams for their family's future, teaching a daughter how to swim so she'd always be safe.

It was about that age when I introduced a new tradition to Wit I had begun with her brother, only it went by a different name:

Daddy-Daughter Day. Every Thursday, we would leave the house early and go to a nearby park or go eat breakfast together. Those special days continued even after school started and into middle school. Thursdays were for Wit and Saturdays for Brayden. My journals indicate that Wit and I did a lot of things during those times together: walking, biking, or sitting in parks listening to birds. I rarely recorded in my journal what we talked about, but she was deeply contemplative from what I can remember, even at an early age. Her wisdom and worldview grew and flourished as she headed into adolescence. I'm so glad that I journaled about some of those times, or I would have lost those memories forever.

When your child dies, the very things you had counted on to make life feel stable are just gone. It feels like you are thrown into the deep end with no life preserver or obnoxious floaties. When Wit died, I found great solace in my journals and hers, remembering our relationship and what it was like to be in her presence. Every hour of those Thursday mornings spent together are priceless to me, even though I don't remember all the specifics. Reading her journals and finding old cards and photos that spark memories is now like a dog-eared page of a good book marking the spot so you can return to it another day. What a life we shared together! I just never expected it to end so soon. When my understanding of the American God of protection and prosperity was crushed, I found myself sitting alone in silence. No longer in the felt presence of God but alone with my memories.

It's in that place—the suffering place, the alone place, the there-are-only-memories-left place—that you begin to realize the memories are the blessing that come out of the suffering. The memories and flashbacks to the good times now gone are not a curse but a grace. The grace of God is very close. In that place, you want to know that God is right here, right now, even though He seems a million miles away during this winter season. My memory testifies that He's not. He is with you every step of the way.

Those Daddy-Daughter days would not have happened without intent. In that same way, God has a communicational intent toward you and me. God is with me, not just on Thursdays, but on every day and in every moment, even if His presence is outside my awareness at times. Although grief has shattered the images I once held onto about the God who responded to complete faith and devotion, the reality is that there is a side to God we only come to know through deep pain and trouble.

It is unfortunate that human religion has muddled things up by only using the mind to connect with God. It's like we try to understand God—who is Spirit and in everything and everyone around us—with just our educated thoughts. Honestly, the connection I made with both Brayden and Wit grew to be more and more sophisticated in our one-on-ones, but when they were very young, we just connected at the heart level.

I remember times when Wit was small and something would frighten her, she would quickly run into my arms for protection, seeking the peace that comes over a daughter holding on tightly to her dad when something mysterious shakes her confidence. Wit did not know what I knew when she was a child. She couldn't see what I saw. But she did know me—my presence and my essence. Since you are God's offspring, His kinship, then you and all His children can tap into these emblems and markers of His presence. Whether someone is a long way from faith or has grown up around authentically spiritual people, they are God's child and He's with them. After a great loss, trauma, or suffering the most authentic way to pick up on the communications of God is from the inner life where God's Spirit lives. Even though He is still a mystery, and you can't see what He sees, you can be open to His presence and essence.

I have come to see that inside our pain and anguish is a comforting God who is not expecting anything but an openness to be together. Those who have suffered losses know that although nothing has changed for anyone else, everything has changed for them. The things they once cared about suddenly seem shallow and unimportant. People will still be running, living life at the speed you once lived, but now that you can see through veils of superficiality and ambition, you realize that you'll have to let them go on. You are experiencing the world at a different pace now. It's a reorientation to life, to your purpose, and to God. It's like waking up out of a zombie-like state of blind ego ambition, unconsciousness, or unawareness, and coming to know that God is offering His presence here and now to the deepest parts of your soul. Sometimes being still while everyone else around you is running is exactly what your soul needs. As Psalm 46:10 says, "Be still, and know that I am God." As horrible as the pain can feel, it is an invitation to yield to this forced stoppage of life, admit powerlessness, and embrace the stillness as a gift.

Covid-19 has reintroduced words like "plague" into everyday speech and caused us to talk about pandemics from the past. Pandemics and plagues throughout the ages have caused fear due to uncertainties and unknowns. The Black Plague is the deadliest pandemic recorded in history. There were three outbreaks of this plague, with the worst being in the mid-fourteenth century.

During this time, an anonymous monk in Northern China wrote a book about the communications of God. The work is titled *The Cloud of Unknowing*. The author says that God is only knowable by love. But he also notes that there is a cloud of unknowing that keeps you from fully seeing and grasping God's communication of love to you. When I think of this cloud of unknowing, I think of its presence during times of suffering and how it is something that's been present for individuals for ages and since sin entered the world. The author describes the cloud of unknowing between you and God in this way:

Diligently persevere until you feel joy in it. For in the beginning it is usual to feel nothing but a kind of darkness about your mind, or as it were, a cloud of unknowing. You will seem to know nothing and to feel nothing except a naked intent toward God in the depths of your being. Try as you might, this darkness and this cloud will remain between you and your God. You will feel frustrated, for your mind will be unable to grasp him.[76]

Looking back, there were so many conversations with Wit where she described this kind of feeling, eerily similar to that quote from all those centuries ago. She would say to me, "God is not speaking," or "I can't feel Him like I used to." Yet that elevated her intentionality to seek God. We all noticed a power, a strength, a wisdom, and an endurance that just seemed to emanate from her. Those characteristics were God's presence guiding and helping her.

Dr. Benjamin R. Doolittle, who is director of Yale's Combined Internal Medicine-Pediatric Residency Program, commented on *The Cloud of Unknowing*, contemplating the relationship between diagnosing a mystery illness and our own connections with God. He wrote this about patients with terminally ill diseases:

The cloud of unknowing refers to the liminal space just prior to full union with God. The author encourages us to "diligently persevere" despite the frustration until, "God in his goodness will bring you to a deep experience of himself." The cloud of unknowing is a dark, uncertain place. ... There are no easy answers.[77]

This vague, uncertain, hazy place is what Wit would journal and talk to me about. In this unknowing and uncertain place, there are no breakthroughs mentally, as nothing can be resolved in that way. Terminal illness means that even science, the accumulated knowledge of the smartest people in the world, can't offer any solid solution. It is a cloud in the mental and liminal space Wit had to enter and live deeply.

If scientists are not able to offer concrete solutions in this kind of situation, it might be wise for the educated religious community and weekend speakers at local churches to admit mystery and uncertainty more readily from the stage. There will be someone every weekend in those churches who is facing the horrors of a diagnosis or complicated uncertainties. Grief, loss, disability, disease, and injustice speak so loudly that they expose things some once believed and now know to be untrue; for example, the belief that the proper level of faith ensures miracles. Countless people you pass by on Sundays are experiencing their own fog of unknowing. It's not something we are eager to talk about because it feels counterproductive to our faith, but as Wit displayed, inside a cloud of ambiguity and uncertainty is an invitation into the mystery of knowing God better. When the fog gets heavy, it's important to remember the solid foundation of God's love for His children.

———————

Tears have a built-in speed or pace to them as they leak over the bottom part of the eyelid and down the cheek. Some days they travel faster than others. They formed and dropped faster as I read again this morning the last Father's Day card I ever received from Wit.

"This next season is more about you than you can anticipate," she wrote in the scribbly style that resembles mine. "I believe you will see yourself differently and be empowered from the inside out to do what has felt too difficult. Fight to overcome and go! I believe in you, Dad. Thank you for believing in me."

In just over fifty days she'd be gone. Looking back, I realize that even then, somehow my faith and believing for a miracle kept me from accepting the inevitability of her situation. Perhaps the experiential eclipse of denial, faith, and the shock of watching my child die kept me from seeing or personally admitting what was really happening.

Compunction is what the old saints used to describe a pain originating from the soul. The ancients taught that compunction hollows out the soul's capacity for God. The more tears that are cried, the more internal space that opens for God.[78] They only spoke of two kinds of tears: higher and lower tears. The lower tears were for the existence of humanity's frailty and distance from God because of sin, and the higher tears stemmed from a greater appreciation of God's love. I think tears can be like little notes found inside fortune cookies at a Chinese restaurant. Each episode of tears carries a message to God from inside the soul of the one crying and sometimes reveals a God message already embedded within, in the deepest part of the soul.

Father's Day cards, birthday cards, notes, and letters are easy ways to pick up on communication from one person to another. But humans are also so complex that we send messages or signs to others in all kinds of verbal and nonverbal ways. Countless people have studied languages over the centuries; the official name for the study of languages is linguistics. This science of language has a subdivision called *semiotics*, which examines how people or groups of people talk to each other before words are formed and how humans create meaning out of life and communicate that meaning to others. Each family, tribe, and group of people—including entire countries—have verbal and nonverbal ways of sending messages to one another. When communicating to a stranger or non-family member, the message-sender must do some extra work. That work starts with sign language or symbols representing the message.

Wit's Father's Day card carried messages to me that you would probably miss. Her message poked my heart as I read it, causing tears that also carried a message. Love does that; it allows Wit and me to converse in a layered and multidimensional way. Of course, my tears while reading the card had mourning components, but they contained much more than that. The card evoked love out of me that is specifically love between me and her. It is still very much alive and present with me now.

God freely chooses to long for us, to be lonely just for us, as I am lonely for just some Wit time. My loneliness for Wit is a kind of echo of God's loneliness for me personally. Wit's card to me will speak to me, carry messages of embedded love to me, for the rest of my life. And it's just one card. I have many cards, notes, emails, and photos—and most importantly, her music—to help me be with her now until we are together again. Yet, in that same way, God has embedded His love and longing for you personally in this moment and in this time. Maybe it's time to allow your heart to admit you long to know God, not just with your mind as if it were possible anyway, but in deeper intimate and spiritual ways.

Pain is an invitation to see God's love as the foundation of all communications that come from God to humanity—to you. The God of the universe communicates presence and love to our elementary minds, on an "Abba-Child" day. He is with you, was at your origin, and is relentless in His love for you, as I am with Wit.

There will always be a "cloud of unknowing" in our relationship with God. We cannot fully understand the God of mystery and that's where faith comes in. Faith is not a tool to be used to get what you want or to keep you from suffering. Faith is what it takes to be open early on and even embody Jesus to others when life gets bad. Faith is to be your response to the suffering and sorrow that hits your life. Maturing in our faith doesn't mean more certainty; it means we must exhibit even more faith.

I still can't get my mind around how a loving God and Father could allow such suffering to come to my daughter. There must be things I don't know. To stay at the table and follow God is like being pushed out of the church nursery's story time with plenty of fish crackers and into a world that is starving and troubled by the terminal loneliness that plagues people's everyday lives. The sooner we embrace the cloud of unknowing rather than try to control or wrangle it to make sense of it, the sooner we can know God deeper and see His great plan at work in us to make all things new.

A relationship with God isn't about trying to figure Him out with your mind; it's about going out with Him in the mornings, getting to know one another more, and growing in love through honest conversations. This is even more true during tough times. If certainty is your goal when it comes to being with God, then the foundation of your relationship with God will crumble. If you are open like a small child to His love, then little by little it will grow and eventually thrive.

You've probably heard someone say, "God told me…" The truth is, they are not necessarily "loopy." It is possible for ordinary people to pick up on these God signs, signals, and moments. But organized religion will struggle to box up and control this aspect of your journey. The first time I remember picking up on a God moment, I was a little boy. I can still remember the surroundings; I remember tears dripping down my face. They were tears of love, higher tears, because I felt sure God and I had made a connection. That's the fascinating thing about communication; it isn't always with words, but if it's from God, it's always with love. God doesn't condemn, rather He invites, and patiently keeps inviting.

The same was true in Wit's relationship with me. Can you imagine her—as a small child—being excited to get out of bed early one day a week to jump in the car with Dad if I condemned her and called out all the things she'd done wrong that week? Our relationship and conversations were rooted in love. Our communication didn't go away when we stopped having official Daddy-Daughter days or when she got married; it was just less frequent. But when it did happen, it was still at the same depth because it was grounded in love. It was not something that required a label or even an official structure; it was time together, spent in heart-to-heart connection. Each additional moment embodied our entire history together. I was at her beginning, her birth, just feet away when she passed through the veil; our love was the unbreakable bond. It still is! God knows your beginning and will be present—even if it's in a cloud of unknowing—on your worst days and bring you through to new creation.

It's impossible for me to explain how God communicates to you. I do not presume to know what God is communicating to you right now. God permeates thinking in a way you might not even be aware of. Sometimes He communicates through actual signs that you can see with your eyes in the physical space around you, and you just know it was something between God and you. Other times, it's through the moments felt or memories remembered. Every living being, including you, has a communal core with God—it's a place much deeper than your thoughts. Even non-religious, brilliant thinkers like Albert Einstein and the scientists trying to uncover the mystery of Hodgkin's Lymphoma—and even confused dads trying to survive the loss of their daughters—have this capacity to decipher their belief or unbelief.

Richard Dawkins, a brilliant communicator and vocal evangelist for atheism who started out as a zoologist, proclaims with certainty that God is only imaginary. Few can touch Dawkins's intellect, especially by academic standards. He is well read and passionate about disproving the existence of God. In *The God Delusion,* a book I've read cover to cover, he leads off his most explicit treatise against religion by quoting Einstein. In the book, Dawkins is frustrated because Christians have taken Einstein out of context when it comes to his belief in a personal, communicating God. Dawkins uses Einstein's own words to prove his point:

> *It was, of course, a lie what you read about my religious convictions, a lie which is being systemically repeated. I do not believe in a personal God and I have never denied this but have expressed it clearly. If something is in me which can be called religious then it is the unbounded admiration for the structure of the world so far as our science can reveal it.*[79]

Dawkins in his self-declared war on religion reveals the kind of "thought" I'm talking about when it comes to God communicating with individuals. He asserts that believing in God is delusional because there is no evidence. Yet, what better way for God to communicate to Albert Einstein than through the structure of the universe? His theory of relativity revolutionized our understanding of gravity, time, space, and the universe as a whole. Dawkins inadvertently confirms this truth. Regardless of the depth and breadth of one's intellect, they'll never be able to get to concrete evidence because the whole universe is created with mystery. This is why we have the discipline of science—there are mysteries that need exploring. In other words, many things exist that we don't fully understand. Therefore, we must research those things.

Pneumiotics is a blended word I created to describe this scenario with Einstein. Built into everyone's life experience are signs, moments, and sufferings or other experiences that awaken one to the reality of God. *Pneuma* means spirit and *semiotics* is the language before vocabulary words are used. The ultimate goal of *pneumiotics* is to more fully embrace the mystery of the Trinity by elevating the awareness that They are already talking to us by the Spirit. Before Wit could even form words and sentences, she still came to know me as Dad. The same is true for everyone since God begins His communicating to you without using words.

I also use the term *pneumiotics* to point to personalized God moments in the human condition. These moments that seem to merge the spiritual and the physical allow for the opportunity to release our fullest potential for living in God and find personal peace. I have come to see that God communicates individually to people, including through nature and their surroundings, to help them deal with suffering. This allows us to transform our pain and not transmit it to those around us. God's presence alone gives an opportunity for our transformation and empowerment.

God has a communicational intent toward you. In the first few lines of John's Gospel account, he even calls Jesus "the Word."[80] *Pneumiotics* suggests that in the mystery and uncertainty of whatever is surrounding you—beauty or suffering—your awareness of God is being elevated. God has embedded in your life experience opportunities for you to pick up signals of His love and abiding Spirit's presence in and around you. Regardless of what you experience, by diving beneath the noise and busyness in your life, you will come to the awareness that God is there. These moments or occasions are for you to discern and interpret personally but they are not any less legitimate than those in the Bible we read about. Most often for me, He is there in silence but I am keenly aware of His presence.

It's easy to live unaware or unconsciously when things are going well for you, promotions are happening, and there's no pain in your life. But when the bad times come, and they will, the heart and mind become more dilated and open to God and His presence. Wit's suffering and now my own grief have awakened me to attributes of God I didn't know existed. I realized that I know much less than I thought I did, but at the same time, I have become a deeper, more in-touch person.

God moments are often recognizable in music, movies, and even in cathedrals or church services, as they can move us emotionally and help open up our souls. Moments filled with music, imagination, beauty, silence, intuition, or physical exercise can produce renewed spiritual energy or an awakened heart. But whether it's a Father's Day cookout celebration or a quick hug shared between a father and daughter, no one can ever hold onto a moment. Moments are precious but quickly gone. The challenge comes in interpreting or translating what has been experienced in that significant moment, recognizing these small threads of the larger story in your life.

Pneumiotics happened to me as heavy tears raced down my cheeks reading a Father's Day card. It was not only a card with heartfelt words written from Wit that spoke to me on that Father's Day, but the words still encourage me today, as I've looked at it several times in the writing of this book. Did God inspire her words and symbols on the card that day? Is it God being my Father in my pain now as I was Wit's earthly father in her pain?

Thoughts and moments can carry messages from God to you but there are also signs that convey a message to the mind from the outside. The science of *semiotics* is the language before vocabulary words are used. It is a sign by which we know something more than before the sign occurred to us. By it we grow in knowledge. A sign is something that stands out to someone personally as a message carrying curiosity or wonder. A bird or a deer will mean something completely different to me and Wit than it does to you. I believe the animals carry little sacred acknowledgments of my kinship with Wit and with God. We are all family. There's no way I'd be able to prove it to Dawkins, but when you're just family and understand it through *pneumiotics*, it doesn't have to rise to that level of documentation. It's between me and God now that Wit is not in this physical space and time, but I'm open to having a message conveyed to me, even if it means tears dropping from my eyes.

Wit's Father's Day card now seems like a sign to me. Dawkins might say this is "sentimental coincidence" caused by my severe suffering. But Dawkins represents not just a different mindset but a different worldview—the worldview where intellect is greater than God and one in which faith is for weak-minded, uneducated dimwits. "Dimwit" is a noun and an informal way of calling someone a stupid person.[81] The origin of the word "dimwit" meant someone of low intelligence, a slow-witted person. That means that if you are a "witted" person, then you are bright and intelligent as opposed to "dim witted." I like to think that those who have known Wit or those reading her story have become "Witted" and see God from a different place.

> *Think of it this way: who knows what is really going on inside a person, except the spirit of the person which is inside them? Well, it's like that with God. Nobody knows what is going on inside God except God's spirit.*[82]

God's abiding presence, as promised to us by Jesus, dwells inside us to help carry or point to these messages already embedded into our human experience. Our communal core, our wit, becomes empowered and enlightened so we don't live as spiritual dimwits. Even the things that cause tears to slide down your face can deliver a fresh understanding of God's love as you remember the suffering God in the first century.

Realizing that these signs, moments, and sufferings carry God's love for me is a step toward surrendering to the reality that Wit is gone. I can't change that, even though our prayers called for things to change for four years. This is the hard part for people who are devout and religious but unawake to the actions of God's Spirit in their soul. Relinquishing control, conceding that God chose not to do anything to change your circumstance, is the only way to cope with uncertainty.

––––––––––

This past Christmas season, before my granddaughter Blake turned two, Blake and I were both on the floor of her room playing "nighty night." It was so much fun as she kept wanting us to lie down on the floor in front of her crib and pretend we were going to sleep. We spent most of that time hugging and laughing, as she would dive on top of me and then I would move a stuffed animal all over her face, snuggling and tickling her. She would suddenly fall down on her stuffed animal, and I would ask, "You okay?" To which she would grin and say, "I'm okay!" Then she would jump up and say, "You okay?" Then she would quickly follow with her own answer, "I'm okay." And then she would signal me to fall. So, from a sitting position I would suddenly fall over, and she would ask, "You okay?" And I would smile and say, "I'm okay." I've never laughed so hard.

The bond and the communication between us grow exponentially every visit. I am more complex than she knows, and it'll be years before she knows that I have two doctorate degrees and can talk naturally about semiotics, post-structuralism, epistemology, and pneumiotics. But that doesn't matter to our relationship. After I caught on to her new game of falling over and then asking, "You okay?" we established a bond and relationship with each other that continues deepening. Our relationship has grown so much that she now calls me, "Poppa!"

I am like Blake when it comes to God. Even though I have decades of graduate work on the topic of God, I am a toddler when it comes to certainty. I know very little, but I know God is here on the floor with me as I pray and grieve the loss of the most precious thing in the world to me, my baby girl. Some days I let Him know "I'm not okay." But He doesn't flinch or leave and seems okay with my honesty.

Stuffed into one of Wit's spiral journals was a poem she wrote that, as far as I know, was never put to music. It flies in the face of the thought that God was not with her in her pain and suffering, the song/poem is called "My Keeper."

> *It's never been so dark, and I've never felt so safe.*
> *Broken down in my pain, You'll hold me and make me whole.*
> *When life betrayed me, You called me Your own.*
> *Tuck me in tonight. Keep me safe. This is home.*
> *There is no distance His arms won't reach.*
> *No frequency louder than His speech.*
> *He spares no expense. He goes the distance.*
> *No darkness could stand.*
> *No power of hell force His hand.*
> *The rock, steady and strong, remains through it all.*
> *I've got nothing if You're not real.*
> *You're the reason for the song.*
> *The hope within the storm.*
> *Grace and beauty are mine.*
> *The sweetest things defeat the bitterness of hell.*

I am continually awed by her wisdom to seek God even when she didn't understand Him, her integrity to trust in her relationship with God even in the storm, and her tenacity to continue walking into the mystery and leading others to do the same.

Uncertainty—about a sickness, a decision, a relationship, or even about God—is like a heavy fog that can descend without warning. It's so heavy that all you can do is see a few steps in front of you. Even if you had the brightest light to shine in front of you, the fog would swallow up its beams. Surrender, relinquishing control, and giving up shallow religious explanations is the path of authentic spirituality and a way to step into the mystery fully present.

Wit was no longer a kid, wearing swim floaties to the pool, but a grown-up when she wrote the Father's Day card to me and this poem that she never told anyone about. She had an ongoing private correspondence with the Eternal One. And it wasn't one-way communication if you examine her words. "I've never felt so safe. … You'll hold me and make me whole. When life betrayed me, You called me Your own." The sheep follow His voice. He led her out, and she followed. He led her beyond time. Those who knew her personally know she was always specifically honest. The amazing thing to me is that her God moments as she journaled her way through cancer now become signs and moments that help me endure my grief and integrate it into a future I never wanted or expected. God was there with her, He's here with me now, and He's there with you too, communicating in a way only you would know.

WISDOM MOMENT

List any spiritual insights or growth thoughts you had as you read the chapter. Have you ever picked up on a sign, a moment, or a suffering that God might use to communicate to you? If so, explain it briefly.

INTEGRITY MOMENT

Describe a particularly difficult time or suffering that you endured in the past. Examine it. How old were you? What was the dominant emotion attached to it? Think deeply about that in relationship to the concept of uncertainty and having to trust God.

TENACITY MOMENT

When a great trial or suffering falls upon you, you will not find peace in the idea of a God but only in your relationship with that God. Write out one private paragraph describing exactly where you are with God in this moment.

CHAPTER 10
TOO DEEP FOR WORDS

In the beginning there was You. In the middle, there was You.
And in the end, God, there will be You—You and me.

—Wit

The thick, heavy gravel crunched under our feet as Wit and I walked
together. We were headed down a long hill toward a summer camp on
the lake, where she'd be singing and sharing stories. The July heat clung
to us, even though it was nearly 8:00 p.m. Wit sang to a group of teens
who were closer to the third grade than college, "In the beginning, there
was You. In the middle, there was You. And in the end, God, there will
be You, You and me."

"In the beginning it was you," she wrote. "God, You saw me, You know
me, You purposed me. In the middle there was You. You've been helping
me to find my way little by little, whether I knew You were there or not."
Then she slams the ending with breathtaking maturity for a song writer
and young woman: "In the end God there will be You! Just You and me!"

Just a huge statement from a young woman writing those lyrics, not
even diagnosed with cancer at that point: "In the end, God, it will be just

You and me." It gets at the biggest questions that underlie all our lives. Questions we rarely verbalize with others, such as, "Where did I come from? Where am I going?" In the young, it shows up in questions like these: "Do you see me? Do I matter? To anyone? Am I normal? Do I fit into the group?"

Wit faced her insecurities early on in life and that theme emerged as she shared a message at the camp that evening. She sang and worshiped her heart out as she wove in stories and insights from her own life. Later she posted an excerpt from her story on Instagram.

> *Spent a good amount of my life believing the lie that I'm not enough. Always lacking and always questioning. It goes all the way back for me. Never good enough. Never skinny enough. Never smart enough. Insecurity is a prison. I'm not there yet, but the accusing voice in my head is getting quieter. I can hear the words "you're enough" so much clearer now. I can look at the people around me and really see them and there's so much beauty. Stop listening to the lie and start believing you're kind of a big deal.* [83]

There was a groan present in her words that night and in her post later. Groans are the way you can pick up on an adult struggling with the big questions of life. The way of Jesus included groaning, suffering, pain, betrayals of all kinds, and then death itself. This is a good indicator that our story will contain all these elements in some way too. As Paul wrote in his letter to the church in Rome, "We know that the whole creation has been groaning as in the pains of childbirth right up to the present time." [84]

The recent tendency by some well-meaning American Christians to tell their spiritual story without the deep groans of emotional or relational pain, uncertainty, or struggle hurts the next generation by leaving them with false expectations. Christian, pre-Christian, or never

Christian people experience deep inward groans and go out of their way to avoid the big questions of life more often than most would admit.

Human beings are wired to be the heroes of their own stories. Since people come to know us by our stories—and we are the strong and invincible heroes of our own stories—we must edit them so that we do not appear as weak or different from the rest of the crowd. When we tell our stories, we reveal the parts we want people to see and perceive about who we are. More often than not, we leave out the groans in our lives. Groans of rebellious teenagers at home disrupting the life we thought we might have. Groans of addicted family members or difficult relational challenges. Groans over our aging parents. Spiritual fathers and mothers should help correct this by sharing the challenging parts of our lives and helping those who follow after us have a fuller, more comprehensive view of just how challenging this life can be. We should talk about the spaces where it seemed that God helped us, but we also need to talk about the spaces where it seems He wasn't much help.

Name a person in the Bible who never suffered a trauma or suffered in body or spirit. I can't tell you how many times I have been grateful for the testimonies of struggle from almost every biblical character mentioned—not just Job! Shockingly, after Jesus' death and resurrection, every one of His disciples, both men and women, still suffered horribly. The miracles that show up around them, for the most part, seem to be for everyone but them. I think our art for avoidance and our desire to be distracted have reached such a magnitude that we often fall into the trap of editing out the groans and troubles of those who have lived before, which prevents us from living in personal awareness of the prevalence of suffering.

Knowing someone's groans is a sign that you're in community. By community, I don't mean just showing up once a week to be inspired by a message and drinking some coffee in the same room with other people keeping their groans to themselves too. I'm not talking about oversharing with everyone in your church of course, but integrating your full story—groans and all—in a healthy, truth-telling way with a small group of fellow believers who will both listen and share.

One of my family's deepest groans is that God disappointed us and our faith theology let us down. Yet, the reverse is also important to share: the God of Scripture didn't actually let us down, because He never promised us a miracle. One's view of God, theology, may reveal more about their own personal hopes than it does about God. Wit's presence was kind of a big deal; she lit up the camp that evening and stood out; she lived knowing she was totally accepted by God. She wanted those students to know it and to know God would never leave them—even in the end, even if He didn't answer their prayers or give them the experience of feeling Him near.

The two of us often talked about those who seem to live *for* God out of fear or guilt and miss the reality of living *in* God in the here and now. More and more, Wit had found that the best way to live with continual bad news was to live in God. Living *in* instead of just *for* is quite a big difference. Many cults and misguided people have lived *for* God but were very far from the deep truth Wit discovered. Living *for* carries the idea of "I'm doing it because I want to secure my final destination," or indicates a person who is acting out of varying levels of fear and guilt. But living *in* God is to carry out the day's activities, whether mundane or going in for chemotherapy, with an awareness that God is in this moment—even if it's a groan. Living *for* God carries a level of performance: you want to be the hero. Living *in* God carries intimacy and humility: you want to be a vessel. Wit expresses this beautifully in her song "I Was Made":

You're the God of invitation, The Lord of all creation, I open my heart to You.
Cause I was made, I was made to love You, to love You.

And I was made, I was made, to adore You, to adore You.
Your ways are higher, higher than mine. All that You do, is right
and true.
Freely You forgave, freely I will live. I open my heart to You.
Cause I was made, I was made to love You, to love You.
And I was made, I was made, to adore You, to adore You.
In the beginning, there was You. In the middle, there was You.
In the beginning there was You. In the middle, there was You.
And in the end, God, there will be You, You and me, you and me.
Cause I was made, I was made to love You, to love You.
And I was made, I was made, to adore You, to adore You.
There's no one like You God. There's no one like You God.

The worst thing that can happen to a person or to a church is to live with no groan, to live like you have God so figured out that mystery and uncertainty in the face of pain and suffering are not allowed. Paul talks about this idea in detail in his letter to the Romans.

We know that the whole creation has been groaning as in
the pains of childbirth right up to the present time. Not
only so, but we ourselves, who have the firstfruits of the
Spirit, groan inwardly as we wait eagerly for our adoption
to sonship, the redemption of our bodies. For in this hope
we were saved. But hope that is seen is no hope at all. Who
hopes for what they already have? But if we hope for what
we do not yet have, we wait for it patiently. In the same
way, the Spirit helps us in our weakness. We do not know
what we ought to pray for, but the Spirit himself intercedes
for us through wordless groans.[85]

The Spirit is closest when the groanings of our inner life are most pronounced. Creation, including humans, cannot free itself from the ultimate outcome of death and decay. But this very groaning is a sign that new birth is happening. It's as if in our groaning and honesty together, we are birthing a new community that is literally founded on resurrection. This is our hope, and even God's Spirit helps us groan it out. Like a woman who gives birth, you'll never see something new birthed in your life without the presence of groaning. There are no spiritual shortcuts, no kind of prayers, sincere or otherwise, that can detour or bypass the groans.

To live *in* God is to be fully awake to the God who suffered so that He could be close to you and me. There is an implicit universal truth that those who love are in God and those who don't have love, especially for the hurting, are not in God. As Scripture tells us, "if anyone obeys his word, love for God is truly made complete in them. This is how we know we are in him: Whoever claims to live in him must live as Jesus did."[86] Jesus—the suffering Jesus, the eating with the non-devout Jesus, and the identifying with those generally perceived to be the furthest from "living in God" Jesus—came close to those who were physically hurting while He was here on Earth.

We must all be intentional about the way we frame our view of God to include the full picture of Jesus' life. If you try to cut out the suffering, the betrayals, and the loneliness of Jesus' story, then you are only left with the water-walking, miracle-making Jesus. That would create false expectations and extra-biblical theology to include the underlying idea of the American dream that you can get what you want if you try hard enough or have enough faith. The idea "Jesus suffered so that I don't have to, and after His resurrection and ascension, miracles abounded everywhere for everyone" is not a universal or even biblical understanding.

Reflecting God's life—living in God—was Wit's reason for living and I think it should be ours too. Unfortunately, we best reflect the transcendent when this life reveals its fragility and brevity. Who of us wants to sign up to suffer? Often our "standing out" at all usually involves a transcendent crisis. Like losing a daughter at twenty-seven. Although every person's journey is different, our greatest responsibilities come in the moments of our greatest pain.

Wit loved vintage items. Looking at it now, I think she was drawn to things from past eras that still had usefulness. Her private home workspace included an antique roll-top desk with a ninety-nine-year-old file cabinet. They were both full of pictures collected from grandparents, personal journals, music folders, spiral-bound notebooks with crinkled pages and scribbled poetry everywhere. She loved ancient books, art, and movies and would kick off the holiday season each year with her sister-in-law, Heather, by watching the 1944 movie *Meet Me in St. Louis*, starring Judy Garland. She even owned a vintage bicycle—her brother still has it. Wit made these antiques look fresh and useful. People would even say about her, "She's an old soul," when it came to her appreciation of the elder generation and her faith.

In an antique bookstore on Vancouver Island just thirteen months before she died, Wit picked out a book on existentialism for my Father's Day gift. It is the school of thought that concerns the rationalistic explanations of human existence and death and asserts that there is more to life than what you can know by thinking. Existentialism takes on the underlying challenges of human existence and the framework of our lives and experiences. Anxiety and dread, boredom and aloneness, and the feeling of nothingness are all topics existentialists examine. Existentialists ask questions like, What is my real nature? What is the meaning of life? What is death? Is there a God? What happens when I die? What is my greater purpose? The average person will also ask these kinds of questions when faced with a tragedy or major change in our lives.

Nineteenth-century existentialist philosopher Søren Kierkegaard said that when we are faced with apprehension and fear around these topics, we must take a leap of faith—as absurd as that sounds. He posits that faith is not proved objectively but by our experiences. He asserted that the place to find untruth is in trying to follow the crowd thinking or popular mindset and abandoning our personal experiences and responsibility. It is possible for someone who just goes to church, is led to ideas about God, and attends on Christmas and Easter, to become no more than a religious clone of a crowd. Someone who has never sought for themselves a relationship with God has no authentic faith. Something foundational is missing for them. Kierkegaard said, "The crowd in its very concept is the untruth."[87] This indicated that faith is to be personal and that makes it subjective in some ways. The full story is that everyone groans at the bigger questions in life, and you find your own faith—an authentic, biblical, historic faith—when it's God in you.

Sometimes our insecurities, feelings of unworthiness, or feelings of being less than everyone else at the table come because we view ourselves in relation to the crowd's opinion. But you are so much more valuable to God than you know. Wit's life—and yours—is complex, rich with all kinds of nuances, texture, and even difficult parts that don't look very devout. Wit's individuality and devotion to living in relationship with God set her apart. She refused to be in the crowd of untruth and sought the God of mystery, the God of relationship. Her experience with God—just her and God—built the sturdiest foundation for when suffering entered her life. She was not reliant or dependent on others' experiences or interpretations of God; she knew Him, she trusted Him, and she followed Him.

God's view of you is not shaped by your job, how you accomplished this amazing thing, or how you were adored by the crowd. God fully embraces all of you—including the parts you hide and all the groans you try to stifle—and invites you to embrace yourself as fully accepted and loved by Him. It's His Spirit that helps you vocalize your groans.

———————

There's no need to edit out the bad experiences of your story, the mystery and failures present. The groaning in your life is normal and it signifies that you're birthing something eternal. Regardless of how hard you try, you will never be able to eliminate the groan. No amount of positive talking, financial prowess, adoration of crowds, or hard work will lessen the groans. If you can see the whole story, the complete narrative is that in this life you will have pain. When we embrace suffering as part of our story, as something that contributes to greater glory, we enter into a deeper relationship with the Author of all our stories—the Ancient of Days.

People come to know us through the stories we tell. Our stories reflect how we want people to perceive us. And even though all our groans are different, they emanate from the same deep place in the soul. The American dream is, in many ways, anti-gospel in that its goal is to eliminate the groans of life. Trying to have a Christianity without suffering is like trying to have Easter Sunday without Good Friday. What if the next wave of deeper spirituality is a revival of the groan?

The way of Jesus reveals to us that our pain, suffering, and traumas—both great and small—lead us back to an unchangeable God. Too many Christians and churches have left out the groans that come to us in this life. Grieving will take time and expend energy. No one gets over the loss of a sister, daughter, or a spouse, but you can add it to your story and journey through the pain with the hope of seeing them again.

As Scripture says, "he who searches our hearts knows the mind of the Spirit, because the Spirit intercedes for God's people in accordance with the will of God. And we know that in all things God works for the good of those who love him, who have been called according to his purpose."[88] That means Wit's death can even be used for good in your life; that's our sincere prayer. No one wanted to see a miracle outcome more than our family. Even until the last day, Wit was hoping and believing for a miracle. Even though we didn't get the miracle, even as we are still walking the path of grief, we can see Wit's life—all the stories, memories, songs, journal entries, quirks, wisdom, everything—was bound together as a story of worship, suffering, and mystery. God's love was at the center of her story, which nothing could destroy. Paul continued his message in Romans 8 to tell us:

> *What, then, shall we say in response to these things? If God is for us, who can be against us? ... Who shall separate us from the love of Christ? Shall trouble or hardship or persecution or famine or nakedness or danger or sword? As it is written: "For your sake we face death all day long; we are considered as sheep to be slaughtered." No, in all these things we are more than conquerors through him who loved us.*[89]

Did you skim over that? Did you see it? Paul wrote, "If God is for us, who can be against us," then he called out the suffering I'm talking about: "trouble or hardship or persecution or famine or nakedness or danger or sword." He said we are "like sheep to be slaughtered." That doesn't sound anything like winning these days in the American church. Jesus' command to His disciples confirms this message about victory in loss: "For whoever wants to save their life will lose it, but whoever loses their life will find it."[90]

All of life is a suffering, and from a purely American, success-driven mindset, any suffering or pain or discomfort you experience would be a waste. Yet, Wit compelled us to "waste our life"—or in Jesus' words, "lose our life"—to live fully, wholly, completely in Him![91]

Life contains contradictions, conflictions, confusion, and mysteries of all sorts; in this way, we learn to carry our cross. Wit always said, "Truth is a person and is beyond our ability to understand, that we should gaze in wonder and appreciate the mystery. We should try to find the beauty in each episode of trouble." Wit was able to find joy and a song in every season. Her faith was real and authentic and mesmerizing, and her life reflected that. She suffered through the groans of life, praying for a miracle, and she did it in a way that drew her and those around her closer to God.

As I carry my cross, I reflect on what I've lost. I lost the expectations that both my kids would have kids that would play together. I struggled with the questions of: What difference did Wit's death make to anyone? Was her suffering pointless and futile? Why can't we have Thanksgiving with her kids and enjoy a cookout this summer? It's part of what motivated me to share with you her story, all of it. Because the Christian life is more about suffering than it is miracles. It's more about endurance than living life physically pain free. Wit's death and our grief are now being woven into each of our personal histories and the story of us. Wit carried her cross and followed Jesus, and she found eternal life in Him. Life will bring great suffering to you at some point, and it's up to you to decide if you will carry your cross.

———————

Yes, there is mystery in life and your life will not go according to your plans, even your best laid ones. You do not get to write your story and craft your own narrative. You will face trials and setbacks, struggles, and suffering—and those parts of your stories, the groans and momentary afflictions, will achieve a glory and be part of a larger story that we can't even begin to imagine. In all the mystery, the thread of your life is weaving something beautiful. Everything is useful and fruitful and can be used to bless those around you and even the world.

Some churches have mission statements that promise safety and security from pain and suffering if you just have faith. However, these are the very things God uses in our lives, this temporary human condition, to wake us up to His love and our union with Him. Some well-meaning pastors and parents go out of their way to protect people from the big questions in life, but if you never allow the big questions and mysteries to surface, you'll never discover the larger way of living *in* God.

Death is our big, big problem. But our big, big God is our solution. Not the God in heaven, not the God in the crowd at church, but the God in your heart! If our lives are in God, then they are not only meaningful but also fully accepted and embraced by God. Bring the dark parts of your personality to God, knowing He will fully and graciously receive them as worship and offer unconditional love back to you. Bring your groans and all your questions, and in doing so you are demonstrating your value and worth in the here and now. As Psalm 34:18 says, "The Lord is close to the brokenhearted and saves those who are crushed in spirit."

Suffering is the transitional door to a deeper and fuller relationship with God. Your personal groans are just pointing out the opportunity to discover a more authentic, greater understanding of who God is in you, even in your suffering. There will always be signs of contradiction, like how someone who is winning can look and feel like they are losing. We know that a victorious, more-than-a-conqueror winner should not suffer pains and losses, but the Bible shows that we are to be co-sufferers with Jesus. John wrote about this amazing process when he quoted Jesus' own words: "Truly, truly I say to you, unless a grain of wheat falls into the earth and dies, it remains alone; but if it dies, it bears much fruit."[92]

Come on out of the shallow American Christian religious mindset and step into a more fully alive and awakened spirituality by seeing how God is in the midst of it with you while you groan. There is a deeply meaningful and wonderful life available to you if you'll step away from the crowd of untruth, pick up your cross, and offer yourself fully to God, trusting in His goodness. Move from being unconscious and unaware to a place of peace, trusting that all you're going through connects to the larger narrative, not only of what God is doing in you but also what He is doing in all of us.

In the beginning you decided nothing; in the middle you decide everything; in the end you decide nothing; you are powerless. Humility is your only power and suffering is the path we all must walk, but if we are open to it, we can awaken our gifts and travel into the mystery with wonder.

WISDOM MOMENT

Select the story or the lyrics that influenced you the most and rewrite them in your journal. Use this exercise to search for what wisdom is coming to your heart through a specific phrase or a word.

INTEGRITY MOMENT

The drive to talk about Wit's historical presence is that—by normalizing suffering and groans and challenge—when a crisis hits you or your family, God is not blamed but rather even more appreciated. Write out some thoughts that come to mind when you consider the phrase "normalizing suffering."

TENACITY MOMENT

Close your eyes and breathe deeply and slowly. Listen for any groans at work under the surface of your life. Reflect on them by either journaling or talking aloud to God about them.

SURRENDERED AND UNAFRAID

I set my eyes on you and not on sickness, not even the solution. Eyes on you, listening for the voice I know so well. Ready to follow. I will follow where it leads, surrendered and unafraid.

—Wit

The sheets of rain were relentless as Wit and I made our way back from the very last treatment, although neither of us knew it was the last at the time. It was that afternoon she revealed to me she was starting to record the tracks for her second album. As she took over the Bluetooth in my four-door truck, I slipped my iPhone upside down and hit the record button. She was funny about giving me songs in progress, as she was still working on them, adding verses or tags. The clip is about seven minutes of pure amazement as she comments here and there about how she plans to tweak this or that. It was the first time I heard pieces of "Travel On" and "Let It Go."

Only Jesus knows what I feel when I hear her singing. I still find it hard to believe God was okay with not helping this amazing, selfless person to live the normal life most of her friends will live. How do we "Travel On," believing that our best days are in front of us or how can I just "Let It Go"?

James the Just, as they called him, was the brother of Jesus who became the head of the church of Jerusalem. History reports that of all the followers of Jesus, he was tortured and suffered the most, so it's fitting that he is often quoted regarding wisdom. He wrote, "For you know that when your faith is tested, your endurance has a chance to grow. So let it grow, for when your endurance is fully developed, you will be perfect and complete, needing nothing."[93] This is the biblical formula for gaining wisdom, integrity, and tenacity: face the pain, surrendering to what is, and be unafraid so you can endure to the place where time is no more.

The sound of our voices together, the heavy rain hitting the wind-shield, and the foreboding cough that she would carry the rest of her earthly days were all captured forever on that two-hour ride. I am still too emotional to listen to it all the way through, but it provides a memory of a Whitney who was surrendered and unafraid. Any memory of that moment in the car is like a sword piercing my soul.

When Jesus was a young boy going to the temple with His parents, a prophet named Simeon took Jesus in his arms and said to his mother Mary, "This child is destined to cause the falling and rising of many in Israel, and to be a sign that will be spoken against, so that the thoughts of many hearts will be revealed. *And a sword will pierce your own soul too.*"[94]

The Greek word for "pierce", or pass through, in this verse is *dierco-mai*, pronounced dee-err-ko-my; the word for "sword" used here is *rhomphaia* (rom-fah-yeh).[95, 96] The only other time this word for "sword" is used is in the book of Revelation, when the Lord delivers an unwelcome word to the listeners. Essentially, the sword referenced here means Jesus did not belong to Mary but is the Lord's and will be used of the

Lord as the Lord sees fit. It is a message to Mary that she will experience trauma or personal pain so that the glory of the Lord might be seen.[97]

This word is used to lay bare all our expectations within us and align us with the wisdom of God. From the moment Mary agreed to carry the Messiah, the literal "Word of God" within her, she was destined to suffer. From almost losing Wit during the birthing process to the four last years of her life, we pleaded with God for a rescue. Our family's hearts have been pierced by an invisible sword—all our hearts have been split in half.

With just six weeks left on this earth, there was still a song in Wit's heart, but her body was physically succumbing to the disease. I was staring tenacity in the face as I watched her. Her mom was there beside her every day since her lungs had collapsed nearly a year earlier. Darla would clean, cook, and rub Wit's head and neck and shoulders for hours at a time. Her brother and sister-in-law were doing all they could do to be near her by bringing food and running daily errands. Her husband stayed by her side through it all. I saw tenacity translated through human flesh in each of them. Wit and I never spoke of how long she had left; she would just say things like, "It's not good, Dad." Before those last few weeks were upon us, my usual response was, "God will make a way where there seems to be no way." But that statement gave way to, "I know, baby girl, I know."

The house filled with an eerie quiet somewhere in those days when the pain became too much for her to come out and sit on the couch with us. For nine months that couch was the holy place where she'd sit with us and be fully present. Brayden or Heather would come by and give love through camaraderie and presence. Her brother was there in the beginning, and he was with her in the end too. The grandparents, family, and church that had been fervently praying were informed things were not good.

The week we lost her is all a blur. She had suffered so long and hard and had been so courageous, we still didn't expect her to leave us early that morning. Decades ago, I read and subsequently shared with many people that some rabbis propose that the windows of heaven were opened between 3:00 and 5:00 each morning. Since before Wit was born, those were the hours I was up seeking to know God for myself. So, it was no coincidence to me that at 3:33 a.m., her shallow breaths ceased. My fingers fumble to type the words and tears start to fall again.

It is the neverness that is so painful and traumatic—to never get to see her children, never again ride in the car with her, never again listen to a new song with her. However, neverness doesn't mean never-ever! We will see her when we are in the forever place, where there is no time, only the present. We will be together in that way—whatever it is and unknown to us now—forever! We will soon trade neverness for foreverness!

I still see Wit everywhere—when I see a deer, or a bird, or a peony. Wit loved peonies even though you can only get them around the spring, after the long cold winter is over. They arrive in stunning colors of pink, cream, burgundy, white, red, and peach. The fragile peony is a fixture in contemporary and classic bouquets. Like birds and nature altogether, Wit deeply appreciated the beauty of these fragile flowers that were only around for a short time. This thick flower always causes me to pause because she loved them so much. What was it about this flower that drew her to it so passionately, this student of nature? I decided I must learn from the peony, and so I tried. Here is a poem I wrote as I sat with its beauty the year after she was gone.

> *Your leaves are large for just a flower,*
> *stretching up high toward His sky.*
> *I see you not with mind but heart, you flower you.*

I saw you come after cold winters breath,
but why leave so soon after your bloom,
your full beauty no one missed,
nor powerful fragrance, a spicy citrus blend,
with you in the garden, other flowers disappeared.
Not here this year, your beauty and fragrance remained.
We miss you dearly, and know you're there.
Stretch down from time to time, you peony you.
Teach us of beauty and wholeness your new song.
Soften hard hearts with your existence, again this year.

Her life on Earth was too short, and I eagerly and desperately wait for the day I get to be with her again, where flowers only bloom and never die. The fragrance of Wit's life lingers on even now. The way she worshiped God—like the woman who anointed Jesus, wasting her life on Him—still inspires and mystifies me. Her beauty is unmissable.

Wit followed God's voice until the end. Her eyes were on Him. As she wrote in her journal, "I set my eyes on you and not on sickness, not even the solution. Eyes on you, listening for the voice I know so well. Ready to follow. I will follow where it leads, surrendered, and unafraid." Here is my own flesh and blood writing a message to me that she was surrendered and unafraid. I believe she was declaring with her own words that she knew His voice and knew it well. The answer is, yes, I think God was speaking to me through Wit's words and maybe He's even speaking to you. Her song "All In" perfectly captures her spirit of surrender and courage.

Take this hurting heart and heal it.
Take these empty words and fill them.
Take the dark in me and make it light.

I wanna be Yours, all Yours.
Will you make me all Yours God?
Will you make me all Yours?
Will you make me all Yours, I...
I wanna be Yours, all Yours.
Take this melody that I sing,
Take this almost love song and make it.
I'll trade all of me for all of You, I wanna be Yours, all Yours.
Will you make me Yours, all Yours, God?
I wanna be Yours, all Yours.
Will you make me all Yours?
Will you make me all Yours, I...
I wanna be Yours, all Yours.
(repeat)
I'm all in, I'm all in, everything to lose, just You to win.
I'm all in, I'm all in, I'm all in.
I'm all in, I'm all in, everything to lose, just You to win.
I'm all in, I'm all in, I'm all in.

The album led off with a blaring electric guitar, introducing "Light Up." And the last song ends with a contemporary monastic humming that reveals the deeper place from which she lived, created, and worshiped. The music fades completely and the listener is left with only the sound of a young woman who finished her time. I doubt she would have changed a thing about her life if she had been able to do it over again. She lived "All In" on God's plan. We can, like Wit, live surrendered and unafraid when we trust the God of mystery. We need not know or understand the way He moves to follow Him wholeheartedly. That's part of surrendering. That's part of faith.

———————

Wit's purity and congruence as an authentic follower of Jesus make her loss all the more unbearable and unexplainable. Facing the contradiction of a God who did not protect her from an inexplicable blood cancer presents a harsh and rigorous challenge to those left behind. So far time does not look like a healer, only a reminder. I'll never be able to touch your pain and you can only visit mine from a distance. All pain is personal, and you can only touch ours and others' from a distance. But if I can use my pain to help you, even just a little, then Wit is still helping others.

Moving from God's bigger story down to your personal story is something I saw her do often. You can get lost in your anger and waste valuable energy if you try to work your personal pain up to God's bigger story. Wit never worked from her suffering and pain and the unfairness of this disease because, as she would often say, "It won't take you anywhere." She modeled working from God's story of love and coming to be with us down into her own story. She lived in such a way that radiated God's presence in every season from childhood to womanhood.

Surrender to what is now becomes the bottom line. Face the pain, the hurt, and the anger with courage. When you relinquish your control of trying to figure out the whys and tracing down all the what-ifs, you will come to a better place, a more sacred space in the heart where there is no time. This place doesn't exist in your mind, but it's the real you, the deeper you, the best version of you, the you that is eternal and surrenders all pains of the mind and heart to God; it is not offered in weakness or strength but in surrender and trust.

> *In the silence.*
> *In the disappointment.*
> *In the storm.*
> *In the suffering.*
> *In the sorrow.*

In the lament.
In the wailing.
In the questioning.
In the mystery.
He is there.

Wit taught me to be fully present in every season of life, in all the valleys and mountaintops and everywhere in between. For her, that included a song. The song that God put into her heart has traveled the long path of grief with us and helps us "Travel On." Her story and her song continually encourage me to lean into the mystery and to look for deer along the way.

Wit's story is about courage, not cancer; about bravery, not bitterness; about you, and not her. If you were to ask me to communicate in a few sentences the essence of what I'm trying to say, it would be this: Pay attention to the moments, memories, and the music (creativity) around you, for in them are contained the mysteries of life. These things are God's way of allowing you to see Him every day.

Right here and right now, moments are simply occasions or avenues through which God is close, whether you're aware He is or not. They can be moments filled with joy or suffering, but they somehow move your story, your life, forward. Moments almost always associate feelings with them and become actual messages to us.

As Frederick Buechner writes in *A Crazy Holy Grace*, memories are like a room that we can retreat to when we intentionally need to remember.

Every person we have ever known, every place we have
ever seen, everything that has ever happened to us—it all
lives and breathes deep in us somewhere whether we like

it or not, sometimes it doesn't take much to bring it back
to the surface in bits and pieces . . . Times too beautiful to
tell or too terrible.[98]

I have taken you into my "remember room," and we've pulled journals off the shelves, examined stories, and read some of Wit's poetry. Wit's was a life to remember, but so is yours. Whether you're fighting your way through cancer right now, walking with someone who is facing some horrible situation, or searching your soul for meaning, sit down in your "remember room" and look for God. He's there somewhere, even now.

The moments, memories, and music we have from Wit all tell us God is not just present everywhere, but He was present here with us in His adorable daughter. From beginning to end, Wit's life and death unearth a view of His presence and perceived absence through every joy and sorrow. Wit's life invites us to feel the foreverness of God and one another and give it away to all our neighbors.

ACKNOWLEDGMENTS

Darla, like Mary in the Bible, you delivered God's gift through Wit to the world. Only a few moms know the depth of your pain and the courage it takes to face each new day. Thank you for trading your career to raise Wit and Brayden, providing such tireless, abiding love to us all. Your wisdom, integrity, and tenacity to carry on keep Wit and the God who crushed our spirits near us daily. This book would not have happened without you.

Brayden, few knew how you defended and took care of your sister back in the day before she was married. You tenaciously loved and defended your sister and stayed by her side in the suffering, even when it appeared God was nowhere to be found. The two of you together created so many great stories and gave us the best years of our life. I pray Beau will be that kind of brother to Blake.

To Heather, you were not a sister-in-law; you were Wit's only sister. She loved you and the way you cherished Brayden. I know you're just as devastated as if you'd grown up with her but your pain has helped us deal with our own. Thank you for your strength and patience and for bringing Blake and Beau into this world.

To Allen, you never left Wit's side from the diagnosis to the end. I didn't talk much about you in the book, but I could have because you helped Wit realize so many of her dreams. You treated Wit special, made great memories for her and for us too. We miss being close to you and I pray God's best for you in the decades to come and I'm deeply sorry for your loss too.

To Mom and Dad, who prayed for Wit not just some mornings but every morning. I am grateful for your love and support. As you age and prepare for heaven, you have a granddaughter who adored you waiting to welcome you home. Thank you to Darla's mom for your tenacious unwavering prayers and the support you give your daughter now. Thank you to all our family, huge family, who prayed, fasted, and loved to the end. To our close and dear friends in Oklahoma, thank you for loving on Wit and standing with us in our loss.

Thanks to the WSF Board who from diagnosis to the end were on their knees believing with us for a miraculous turnaround and provided a generous sabbatical for us to start our mourning process in private. All of you will forever be a part of our lives. To the pastors and staff at WSF who carried the load of ministry for us during Wit's last year of life and in her loss. Thank you for caring, crying, and holding our hearts in yours. To the congregation of WSF who went "All In" on believing with us for a miracle. To Mike and Sandi Messner, who through it all were a constant source of strength. To all my pastor friends, thank you for every kindness.

To three extraordinary men who stood with me, texted with me, stayed on their knees with me. There's no need to put your names here because you know how grateful I am for your love and care even to this day. You were with me through the death valley and never flinched. You have provided for my family in ways only God knows. Thanks to the friends and board members of ORU who loved on Darla and me and cared for our broken hearts during and after our loss.

Thank you to Wit's God-sent doctor, Dr. Z, for moving Earth and imploring heaven to try to save Wit. Thank you to Kat, you were so special to Wit during those hard treatments and appointments. Wit would be glad to know you read her full story as she was always hoping to be a bright light to help on your path.

To all Wit's friends, too numerous to call out, especially those close girlfriends, you know who you are. Thanks for keeping her memory alive. You'll be with her again one day, I promise.

Thank you to David Docusen, author of *Neighborliness*, who over a cup of coffee asked if I was writing about Wit. Thank you for introducing Wit's story to Esther. Thank you, Esther, for helping get Wit's story out there; I am grateful that you offered up the full force of The Fedd Agency team. Special thanks to my brilliant editor, Tori, who got to know Wit, listened to her music, and pushed on me to get Wit's story picture perfect.

SOURCES

CHAPTER 1

1. Thomas Merton, *The Silent Life* (New York, NY: Farrar, Straus and Giroux, 1999), 38.

2. Ps. 72:17 NLT

3. Is. 53:3

4. Heb. 4

5. Matt. 26:39

6. Matt. 22:37

7. 1 Cor. 11:24 MSG

8. Rom. 12:1-2

9. Annie Dillard, *Teaching a Stone to Talk and Other Expeditions and Encounters* (New York, NY: Harper & Row, 1982), 52-53.

CHAPTER 2

10. Frederick Buechner, *Beyond Words: Daily Readings in the ABC's of Faith* (New York, NY: HarperCollins, 2004), 266.

11. "Vocation (n.)," Online Etymology Dictionary, accessed May 27, 2021, https://www.etymonline.com/word/vocation#etymonline_v_7862.

12. Matt. 10:39

13. Luke 7:20

14. Luke 7:22

15. Luke 7:23 TPT

16. Luke 19:41-44

17. Mark 15:33-34 NLT

18. Eccles. 3:1,4

19. John 16:33

CHAPTER 3

20. Dietrich Bonhoeffer, *Meditations on the Cross*, ed. Manfred Weber, trans. Douglas W. Stott (Louisville, KY: Westminster John Knox Press, 1998), 25.

21. John 9:2

22. John 14:9; Luke 9:48; 18:16

23. John 9:3

24. Diane Langberg, *Suffering and the Heart of God: How Trauma Destroys and Christ Restores* (Greensboro, NC: New Growth Press, 2015), 55.

25. Dietrich Bonhoeffer, *Letters and Papers from Prison*, ed. Eberhard Bethge (New York, NY: SCM Press, 1971), 10.

26. John 16:7

27. Matt. 7:24-25 NLT

28. Prov. 25:2

29. Ps. 91:9-11

30. Ps. 91:14-16

31. Dietrich Bonhoeffer, *Meditations on the Cross*, 25.

CHAPTER 4

32. Maryanne Stevens, ed., *Reconstructing the Christ Symbol: Essays in Feminist Christology* (Eugene, OR: Wipf & Stock, 2004), 75.

33. "Angel of Grief (Cimitero Degli Stranieri Acattolici Al Testaccio): Art in the Christian Tradition." November 27, 2020, https://diglib.library.vanderbilt.edu/act-imagelink.pl?RC=54142.

34. "The Original Angel of Grief by William Wetmore Story, Protestant Cemetery, Rome," Walks in Rome (Est. 2001), August 28, 2019, https://www.walksinrome.com/blog/the-angel-of-grief-by-william-wetmore-story-protestant-cemetery-rome.

35. John 11:35

36. John 12:1-7

37. Gen. 3:19

38. John 12:24

39. Matt. 20:16

40. Luke 22:42

41. Heb. 4:14,16 NLT

CHAPTER 5

42. Vincent van Gogh, "638," 638 (642, 506): To Theo van Gogh. Arles, Monday, 9 or Tuesday, 10 July 1888. Vincent van Gogh Letters, July 10, 1888, http://www.vangoghletters.org/vg/letters/let638/letter.html#translation.

43. Matt. 26:61

44. Pastor Rick, "How to Get Through What You're Going Through Intro | Pastor Rick's Daily Hope," YouTube video, 1:26:47, March 12, 2014, https://www.youtube.com/watch?v=gaQ_oTp7tKY.

45. Nisha Zenoff, *The Unspeakable Loss: Hope, Help, and Healing after a Child Dies* (New York, NY: Da Capo Lifelong Press, 2017), 5-6.

46. Nina Siegal, "Van Gogh's Pastoral Days," The New York Times (March 12, 2015), https://www.nytimes.com/2015/03/13/arts/international/van-goghs-pastoral-days.html?smid=url-share.

47. Vincent van Gogh, 220 (219, 190): To Theo van Gogh. The Hague, on or about Sunday, 23 April 1882. Vincent van Gogh Letters, April 23, 1882, http://vangoghletters.org/vg/letters/let220/letter.html.

48. Vincent van Gogh, 294 (295, 253): To Theo van Gogh. The Hague, between about Wednesday, 13 and about Monday, 18 December 1882. Vincent van Gogh Letters, December 18, 1882, http://vangoghletters.org/vg/letters/let294/letter.html.

49. Rainer Metzger and Ingo F. Walther, *Van Gogh: the Complete Paintings* (Germany: Taschen, 2015).

CHAPTER 6

50. C. G. Jung, *Structure and Dynamics of the Psyche*, ed. Sir Herbert Read et al., trans. R. F. C. Hull (Princeton, NJ: Princeton University Press, 1960), 399.

51. Antonio Damasio, *The Strange Order of Things: Life, Feeling, and the Making of Cultures* (New York, NY: Vintage Books, 2019), 140.

52. Georgene G. Eakes, Mary L. Burke, and Margaret A. Hainsworth, "Middle-Range Theory of Chronic Sorrow," *The Journal of Nursing Scholarship* 30, no. 2 (1998): pp. 179-184, https://doi.org/10.1111/j.1547-5069.1998.tb01276.x.

53. Gina Mussio, "9 Things You Didn't Know About the Trevi Fountain," Walks of Italy, April 28, 2014, https://www.walksofitaly.com/blog/art-culture/9-surprising-facts-trevi-fountain-rome#:~:text=1.,the%20fountains%20of%20central%20Rome.

54. "Aqueducts and the Trevi Fountain." Accessed June 10, 2021. https://depts.washington.edu/hrome/Authors/floods/TheTreviFountain/pub_zbarticle_view_printable.html.

CHAPTER 7

55. *O Brother, Where Art Thou* (Walt Disney, 2000).

56. Ibid.

57. Ps.13:1-5 NLT

58. Ps. 88:1-2,9,13,15,17-18 NLT

59. Matt. 6:10

60. John 11:35

CHAPTER 8

61. Aristotle, Thoughts on the Business of Life (Forbes Magazine), accessed June 7, 2021, https://www.forbes.com/quotes/642/.

62. "H8577 - Tannîn - Strong's Hebrew Lexicon (Kjv)," Blue Letter Bible, accessed June 7, 2021, https://www.blueletterbible.org/lexicon/h8577/kjv/wlc/0-1/.

63. Chad Brand et al., eds., *Holman Illustrated Bible Dictionary* (Nashville, TN: Holman Reference, 2003), 155-160.

64. "Marduk (God)." Ancient Mesopotamian Gods and Goddesses. Accessed June 10, 2021. http://oracc.museum.upenn.edu/amgg/listofdeities/marduk/.

65. David Toshio Tsumura. "The Creation Motif in Psalm 74:12–14? A Reappraisal of the Theory of the Dragon Myth." Journal of Biblical Literature 134, no. 3 (2015): 547-55. Accessed December 17, 2020. doi:10.15699/jbl.1343.2015.2780.

66. 1 Cor. 10:13

67. Jas. 1:5 NLT

68. Trey Gowdy, *Doesn't Hurt to Ask: Using the Power of Questions to Successfully Communicate, Connect, and Persuade* (New York, NY: Random House, 2020), 124-125.

69. Isa. 54:17 NKJV

70. Eph. 6:1-3

71. J. R. R. Tolkien, *The Hobbit* (New York, NY: Houghton Mifflin Company, 2012), 235.

72. Amos Tversky and Daniel Kahneman, "Extensional versus Intuitive Reasoning: The Conjunction Fallacy in Intuitive Reasoning," in *Heuristics and Biases: The Psychology of Intuitive Judgement*, ed. Thomas Gilovich, Dale W. Griffin, and Daniel Kahneman (Cambridge: Cambridge University Press, 2002), pp. 19-48.

73. Elisabeth Powell, "A Literature of Modern Suffering: Suffering in the Work of Feodor Dostoevsky, Albert Camus and Milan Kundera," Western Sydney University ResearchDirect, March 2007, http://handle.uws.edu.au:8081/1959.7/15716.

74. Sigrid Goldiner, "Medicine in the Middle Ages," metmuseum.org (The Metropolitan Museum of Art, January 2012), https://www.metmuseum.org/toah/hd/medm/hd_medm.htm.

75. Matt. 18:3

CHAPTER 9

76. William Johnston, ed., *The Cloud of Unknowing and the Privy of Counseling* (New York, NY: Image Books, 2005), 40.

77. Benjamin R. Doolittle, "The Cloud of the Unknowing and the Conundrum of Medical Diagnosis," Conference on Medicine and Religion, October 3, 2018, http://www.medicineandreligion.com/october-blog---benjamin-doolittle/the-cloud-of-the-unknowing-and-the-conundrum-of-medical-diagnosis.

78. Irenee Hausherr, *Penthos: The Doctrine of Compunction in the Christian East*, trans. Anselm Hufstader (Kalamazoo, MI: Cistercian Publications, 1982).

79. Richard Dawkins, *The God Delusion* (New York, NY: Mariner Books, 2008), 36.

80. John 1:1-4

81. "Dimwit," Merriam-Webster, accessed June 7, 2021, https://www.merriam-webster.com/dictionary/dimwit.

82. N. T. Wright, The Kingdom New Testament: A Contemporary Translation. New York: Harper One, 2012.

CHAPTER 10

83. Whitney Vesterfelt (@whitneyvesterfelt), "Spent a good amount of my life believing the lie that I'm not enough. Always lacking and always questioning," Instagram photo, April 23, 2018, https://www.instagram.com/p/Bh742AFng5j/.

84. Rom. 8:22

85. Rom. 8:22-26

86. 1 John 2:5-6

87. Soren Kierkegaard, *Provocations: Spiritual Writings of Kierkegaard*, ed. Charles E. Moore (Walden, NY: Plough Publishing House, 2014), xxix.

88. Rom. 8:27-28

89. Rom. 8:31,35-37

90. Matt. 16:25

91. Matt. 10:39

92. John 12:24 NASB

CONCLUSION

93. Jas. 1:3-4 NLT

94. Luke 2:34-35, emphasis added

95. "G1330 - Dierchomai - Strong's Greek Lexicon (Kjv)," Blue Letter Bible, accessed June 8, 2021, https://www.blueletterbible.org/lexicon/g1330/kjv/tr/0-1/.

96. "G4501 - Rhomphaia - Strong's Greek Lexicon (Kjv)," Blue Letter Bible, accessed June 8, 2021, https://www.blueletterbible.org/lexicon/g4501/kjv/tr/0-1/.

97. Basil Burns, "THE PRESENTATION 2014 - 'A Sword Will Do WHAT?'" Freeing the Captives, February 2, 2014, https://freeingthecaptives.wordpress.com/2014/02/02/the-presentation-2014-a-sword-will-do-what/.

98. Frederick Buechner, *A Crazy, Holy Grace: The Healing Power of Pain and Memory: Participant Guide* (Nashville, TN: Abingdon Press, 2018), 58.